It's Called Presenting, Not Talking Out Loud

A Quick, Strategic Guide for Effective Presentations

By

Al Golzari

For bulk discounts to corporations and universities, please inquire at www.presentingbook.com

Gift versions are also available for teams, with custom inside matter, such as a letter from the CEO, President, etc.

Corporate logos on the front cover (within the existing, available white space) are also available with an exclusive gift version.

INTRODUCTION

The purpose of this guide is relatively simple and modest. The focus here is not on general business communications but rather on presentations.

The motivation came from my desire to help, and the belief that I bring something unique to the table. Something that makes sense – for the majority of us. In a natural way.

I don't have any formal training in communications aside from taking a communications course while I was pursuing my MBA. Nor do I come from the consulting, human resources or career coaching worlds. My background is actually in consumer product development and sourcing, in addition to adjunct teaching in marketing, innovation/entrepreneurship, and international business.

However, I do consider myself a pretty solid natural presenter. I'm a talker, not a writer, and have always been told I had the "gift of gab."

I accidentally fell into teaching business communications at the graduate level a few years ago. I'm a marketing guy and, in many schools, the business communications program is housed within the marketing department. I had innocently reached out to the marketing chair of one of the universities

I'm affiliated with and asked if he needed me to teach additional marketing classes the upcoming semester. He asked if I would be willing to teach a few sections of business communications since there were some immediate vacancies at the time. I briefly hesitated but figured I'd go for the challenge.

As with anything new, I needed to iron out the wrinkles. It turns out, though, I was pretty good at teaching business communications. My approach was pragmatic – take my natural presentation skills and marry them with all of the lessons I had learned about effective business communications from my industry experience.

Something inherently seemed to be working, and the students generally seemed to be responding positively. Some of the most insightful feedback I've received have been comments like:

"I didn't think I was going to get anything out of this and saw it was another required, fluffy communications class and a waste of my time, but you really taught me some useful things."

"Your assignments, specifically, gave me the preparation I needed to land the job I wanted."

So I stayed with it, serving at the pleasure of the marketing chair and business communications program director.

Early on, I started to realize how much I already knew but never quite had the opportunity to share. It turned out that these business communication courses were precisely that missing forum. With my corporate experience and some careful thought came an opportunity to introduce my own assignments, strategies and techniques. Some of these were, and still might be, a bit unorthodox, but they work. This is what I'd like to share with you.

This guide – I'm purposely calling it a "guide" and not a book— is not an attempt at yet another communications text. There are enough of those. I'm also not trying to compete with any of those texts.

My background in marketing and innovation has prepared me well enough to ensure that I differentiate myself among the competition. What I'm providing you is a handy, user-friendly guide to use in industry or school.

You'll find this more strategic than tactical, although I blend both at times. That doesn't mean it isn't practical; it very much is. In other words, if you first follow the principles I've laid out in this guide and apply them, no matter your skill level, I guarantee you will become a more effective speaker and presenter.

Whether you need to brush up on your industry skills, or enrolled in a communications course or school in general, or if you are preparing for an important presentation or speech, you can rely on this guide as a handy reference. I am of the firm belief that public speaking and presenting is an art, not a science. And while some of us have natural speaking abilities, we ALL need practice from time-to-time.

I'm rooting for you...

WHO THIS GUIDEBOOK IS FOR

This guide is for anyone doing presentations and wants to:

- Improve
- Reinforce
- Build Confidence

The goal has been to create a guidebook that cuts out all of the fat and unnecessary theory for those who just need the keys. Some chapters are approximately only a page to a page-and-a-half, by design.

If you're a practitioner in any industry and need to make presentations, this guidebook can help.

If you're a student enrolled in a communications course, my hope is that you can treat this guidebook as a supplement to the other materials your instructor has assigned. And it's my sincere hope that some instructors would adopt this guide as part of their curriculum.

I wanted to simplify and make this as practical and user-friendly as possible. As with all texts, you can read this from start to finish, and I hope since there aren't many pages, you'll find it all concise and useful. If you were to read this from start to finish, it's probably about a 90-minute read. However, you can also specifically flip to what you may need.

There's a short bibliography section at the end of this guide. Where I borrowed, I did my very best to give credit where credit is due. But for the most part, the content in this guide comes from my instinct and experience. And I hope that helps add greater value.

TABLE OF CONTENTS

This guide is divided into two parts: strategy and execution.

STRATEGY:

EXECUTION:

CHAPTER ONE | THE THREE C'S

I came up with the three C's – Conviction. Clarity. Context – a few years ago, after having witnessed many powerful and effective presentations, and equally as many ineffective ones.

CONVICTION

To speak with conviction means to speak with passion. Although passion is a clichéd term, and I hate clichés, it still has value.

Speaking with conviction shows you *own* your content. We'll discuss owning content in a separate chapter. To own your content means you know what you're talking about or, at minimum, you give the impression that you do. Sometimes that is enough. This doesn't mean you always have to be an expert in every facet of the topic you're presenting about, but it does mean that you truly believe in the words you're saying.

I speak from experience; once you lose your audience's attention, you generally never get it back. You really need to ask yourself, "If I'm not enthusiastic, why should the audience be?"

Believe me when I say this: Conviction takes you half way to the finish line in a presentation.

You don't need to scream or jump up and down or do cartwheels, per se. People might think you are crazy.

However, speaking with conviction means that the words that come out of your mouth flow so well and are so strong that they are hard to contest. Whether people agree or not, everyone *respects* what you are saying. Your words are unstoppable.

CLARITY

With all due respect, I find too many people today speak with "marble mouth." You've heard the term. Their words seem a bit garbled. When speaking, they don't finish each word before beginning the next one. I think most people can do something to change that. Enunciate.

I also find that many people speak way too fast. Why exactly? I'm not sure. I have some thoughts, but that's irrelevant to this discussion.

I've travelled to China for business many times over the years. English-speaking Chinese people have often told me that they enjoy speaking to me in English because I don't talk too fast or too slow, and they can continue to enhance their English skills. I'll take the compliment.

When you speak, you should respect the words that come out of your mouth. Why do so many of us wake up in the morning, put on nice clothes to either feel good about ourselves or to impress others, but when it comes to our speech we don't invest nearly as much effort? We put so much energy into the way we look and the latest trends on social media, but we don't concern ourselves nearly as much with how we come across when we speak? I've never understood that. Let's stop making everyone else rich and famous by giving them all of our attention. Let's invest in ourselves a bit.

Speaking with clarity is an investment that lasts a lifetime.

This sounds corny, but the truth is I've never hired someone who was qualified but had marble mouth during an interview. Instead, I've always given people who were well-spoken during an interview a bit more preference, even if they had a slight deficit in experience or a particular skill.

CONTEXT

If you've ever been given feedback that you speak too much (like I have), you may have wondered why. I'm going to guess that you were either slightly bothered by or indifferent to the feedback. I can bet, though, that no one ever mentioned how to help correct that.

To speak with context is to be aware of who your audience is, your surroundings and your end objective. I have a chapter on audience which will further explain. For example, if you are doing a business presentation on sourcing and supply chain, consider how much you can reasonably assume your audience *already knows* and what they *need to know.* Stay within that range. Don't provide unnecessary information.

Furthermore, your tone should rest with whether your audience is comprised of senior or junior executives. Some people are better than others at accomplishing this. Some of us, myself included, need to practice.

This is particularly true when we are passionate about the subject; we can sometimes get lost "in the romance." It's important to keep in mind that not everyone will care about the topic as much as we do. While that may be a bit discouraging at times, it's the truth.

In short, it's important to give your audience what they need—no more, no less.

CHAPTER TWO | ORGANIZATION AND PREPARATION

I've seen many presenters fall short of their own expectations. They put in hours of preparation but end up wondering why their presentations weren't as successful they expected. Often, the answer is misplaced energy. They dedicate hours to designing PowerPoint or Keynote slides, and focus too much on aesthetics— font sizes, graphics, etc. These aspects of presentations are important and necessary, but do not qualify as preparation. They're more technical.

By preparation, I am referring to *strategic aspects* — defining your objective (in case you're not clear), and determining the overall structure to your presentation.

To prepare is to organize. Organization is essential for your ideas to flow in a seamless sequence that *makes sense*. But it doesn't have to be linear. It can, but it doesn't have to be.

The good news is that there are many ways to create and deliver an effective presentation. Movies, songs, and books have structure. So should your presentation. The following sections of this guide discuss the above points in greater detail, focusing on the importance of strategic preparation.

Before you get into the following chapters to better understand each element, you need to come up with a macro-level plan to organize your presentation – and figure out the best plan of attack.

All presentations consist of three basic pieces (I prefer to call them pieces as opposed to sections, because I think that works a little easier in the mind):

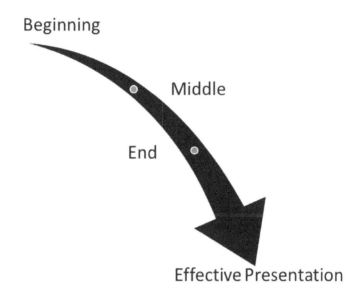

- In the beginning, we have our introduction, which actually can be two parts. There's the opening and the set-up (or preview). You don't always need to have an opening in your introduction, but you may choose to, in order to entice your audience from the very start (assuming that you'll do an effective opening to really engage your listeners). Please refer to the chapter on Presentation Introductions for more. This is our set-up, and there are many ways to set up a presentation.

- In the middle, we have the "meat" of our presentation (the details, to whatever extent those may be).
- In the end, we have our conclusion – where we tie everything together (and sometimes also summarize, depending on the nature of the presentation). And there are chapters throughout this book that are dedicated to each.

So come up with a plan. I'll help you organize this and share some examples but before we do so, here's a quick snapshot of how you should look at this:

Let's break this out into further detail and I'll help you organize what goes into each of these three key areas:

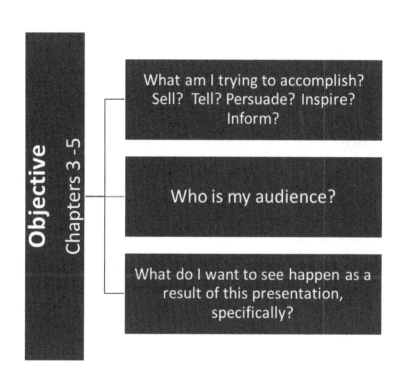

Objective
Chapters 3 -5

What am I trying to accomplish? Sell? Tell? Persuade? Inspire? Inform?

Who is my audience?

What do I want to see happen as a result of this presentation, specifically?

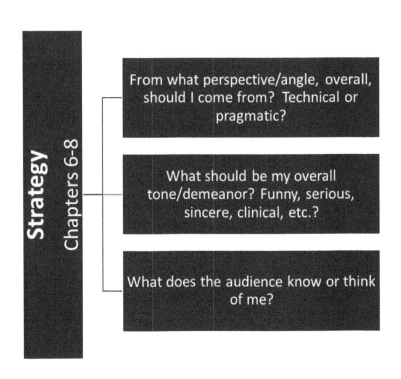

Strategy
Chapters 6-8

From what perspective/angle, overall, should I come from? Technical or pragmatic?

What should be my overall tone/demeanor? Funny, serious, sincere, clinical, etc.?

What does the audience know or think of me?

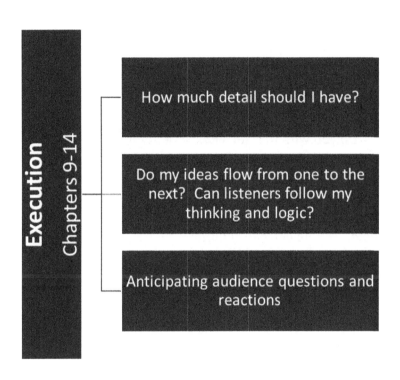

Execution
Chapters 9-14

How much detail should I have?

Do my ideas flow from one to the next? Can listeners follow my thinking and logic?

Anticipating audience questions and reactions

LET'S MAKE A CAKE

One of the most important questions you (hopefully) have on your mind is what is the appropriate balance between the actual content of your presentation and the overall appearance, or "package." In chapter 11, I discuss some tactical issues to be aware of. But that's the execution side of this book. And this is strategic.

To help you with this, let's look at it in terms of making a cake. And for the purpose of this discussion, let's assume you know how, in general, to properly prepare and bake a cake. And let's assume you're hosting some type of dinner party at your home. You have three choices:

1. Focus the majority of your time making the cake really "pretty" with all types of beautiful icing, colors, and other aesthetics but not much time on the cake itself before it goes in the oven.

2. Focus the majority of your time making the cake a really high-quality, incredibly tasty cake. But not worrying all that much on the aesthetics. Maybe you have a very basic icing spread on. Or maybe your cake is so moist

and delicious you don't even bother with an icing or anything like that.

3. Create a pretty good balance between the look and taste of the cake.

What are the consequences of these options? In order of the above:

1. You have a cake that everyone wants a piece of, and they give you great compliments before they get served their slice. But once they bite into it, they're not really impressed. There's nothing wrong with the cake – it's not as though you confused salt with sugar, etc., (remember, you know how to make a cake) but it's just "ok."

2. You have a cake that doesn't necessarily captivate people and you may not receive too many comments at first (yet at the same time doesn't turn them off), but once they bite into a piece they will be so incredibly pleased. Maybe even more than pleased. Perhaps delighted.

3. Your aesthetics and the cake itself more-or-less matched what your guests were expecting.

So what's my point and how does this info help you with your presentation?

Part of the answer rests upon your audience. Which I devote time to in various areas of this book.

But, and you probably know where I'm going with this, try to focus on options 2 and 3, above. Not really option 1. It's not my objective to be judgmental here, because I really want to help you. But I've seen far too many presentations focus on option 1. And not enough on options 2 and 3.

There was so much time spent on beautiful layouts, colorways, fonts, etc. (all fine things, by the way), but the presenter either didn't have that much to say OR they simply didn't do a quality job delivering content. Everyone will be able to tell.

If you go with option 1, again, when your guests are looking at the cake, they are excited. In the same way that your audience will most likely be excited with your title slide and maybe your first few slides. But once you get into the meat of the presentation, there's a good chance you've turned off your audience. In the same way that once your guests bite into their piece of cake, they're kind of not digging it anymore. And looking for a way to place it down on some table in your home and walk away from it.

For general audiences, I'd say go with option 3: create a balance between your aesthetics and content, or "meat" of your presentation.

For more specific, or "serious" audiences, I'd say lean a bit closer to option 2: don't provide too much "razzle-dazzle." Just have a clean presentation where CONTENT rules.

STRUCTURING YOUR PRESENTATION

If you really think about it, while there is probably only one objective to each presentation, there are several ways (strategy) to do it. And once you've come up with at least more than one strategy, the ways you can execute also increase.

One further thing (which I have a chapter devoted to), your audience will most likely also play a role in your decision-making.

Think of having to clean a home, top-to-bottom. Let's say this is a single-family house, 3-4 bedrooms, 2 baths, living room, dining room, kitchen, and a basement.

If you need to clean the house because you're selling it, perhaps you'll want to hire a professional crew. If you're cleaning just for the sake of cleaning, perhaps you'll do it yourself.

Here's an example:

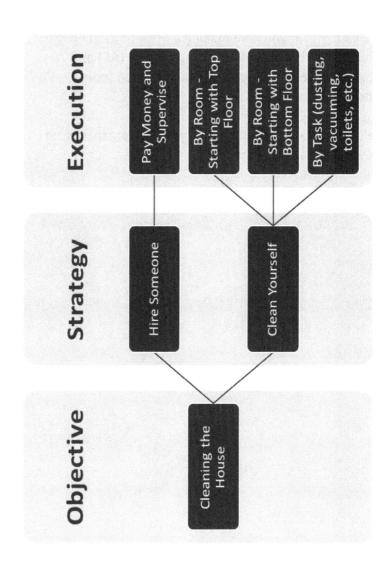

Objective → Strategy → Execution

Objective: Cleaning the House

Strategy:
- Hire Someone
- Clean Yourself

Execution:
- Pay Money and Supervise
- By Room - Starting with Top Floor
- By Room - Starting with Bottom Floor
- By Task (dusting, vacuuming, toilets, etc.)

Now let's translate this into what it means for a presentation.

Let's say that you'll be making a presentation on the difference between alternating current (AC) and direct current (DC) to a general audience (non-technical people).

Here are some ways in which you may organize your overall presentation:

Option 1:

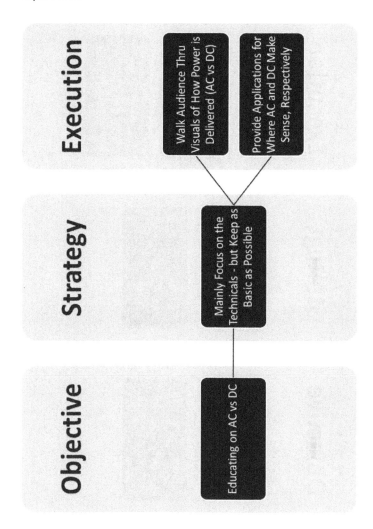

Option 2:

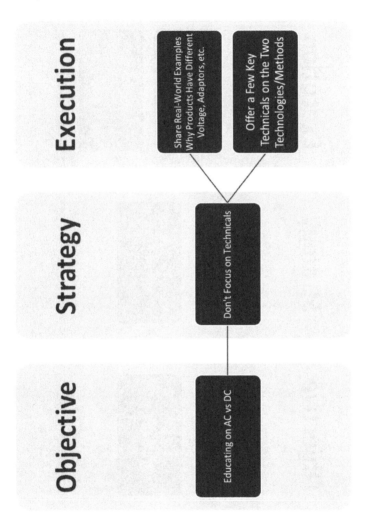

Objective

Educating on AC vs DC

Strategy

Don't Focus on Technicals

Execution

Share Real-World Examples Why Products Have Different Voltage, Adaptors, etc.

Offer a Few Key Technicals on the Two Technologies/Methods

Option 3:

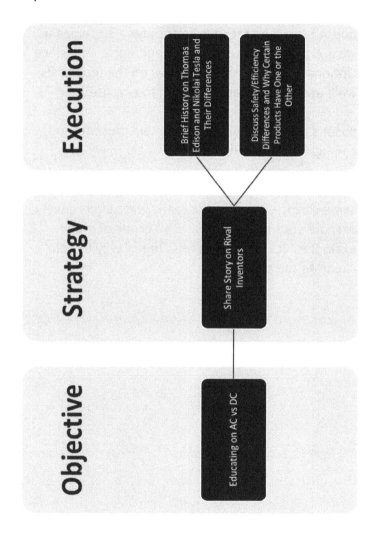

Execution

Brief History on Thomas Edison and Nikolai Tesla and Their Differences

Discuss Safety/Efficiency Differences and Why Certain Products Have One or the Other

Strategy

Share Story on Rival Inventors

Objective

Educating on AC vs DC

Let's say we now want to build out a presentation (with slides) and we've landed on a strategy that doesn't focus on technical attributes – since again, we are presenting to a general audience. And since Options 2 and 3 both don't focus on the technicals, we'll use a combination of both to execute.

So let's construct this with a sample presentation, coming from Options 2 and 3.

Of course, since presenting is both ART as well as some science, there are so many ways to creatively execute your presentation. This is one of many examples. It was done in this "basic" way to help illustrate the pedagogy.

Introduction Slide 1 (BEGINNING): I start with the "IMAGINE" introduction technique (Chapter 10):

Imagine...(PAUSE)...Imagine living in a world where there was no electricity, and all you had when the sun went down was candle power?

Introduction Slide 2 (BEGINNING):

Think of how different your life would be without the light bulb. But this isn't about the light bulb, per se, – it's more about imagining your life without electricity.

Slide 3 (BEGINNING):

More specifically, AC/DC – alternating vs direct current.

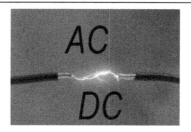

Alternating **C**urrent

vs.

Direct **C**urrent

Slide 4 (TRANSITION TO MIDDLE):

But to tell you about AC vs. DC, I first need to tell you about two interesting people. Pioneers of their time. Thomas Edison and Nikolai Tesla. They were like the Steve Jobs and Bill Gates of their time. Their stories are quite fascinating. The saga of AC/DC was riddled with passion, partnership, politics, scandal, and eventual loathing for each other. I think the only thing missing from this tale was sex.

Slide 5 (MIDDLE):

The difference between AC and DC, for all of us non-technical people (myself included), think of it like these illustrations. DC, or direct current, flows in a straight line. AC, or alternating current, has an ebb and flow pattern.

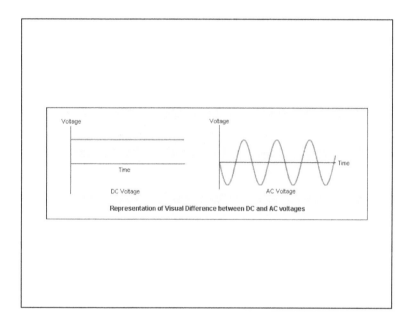

Representation of Visual Difference between DC and AC voltages

Slide 6 (MIDDLE):

In DC, you're carrying electricity, essentially in a straight line, with generators, to the destination. In AC, you're doing something similar, but you'll notice with the areas circled, there are transformers. Smaller amounts of electricity are needed from the source – and can be passed through, and then converted. In both cases, the total electrical power is the same.

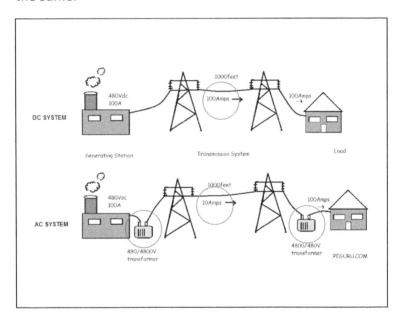

Slide 7 (MIDDLE):

But as mentioned, the story of AC and DC is like a classic soap-opera. Edison took every opportunity he could, to try and undermine Tesla's AC model. Wanting to demonstrate how AC was far more unsafe to DC, Edison went so far and took advantage of the electrocution of Topsy the Elephant, claiming that the suffering of this popular circus elephant was due to AC.

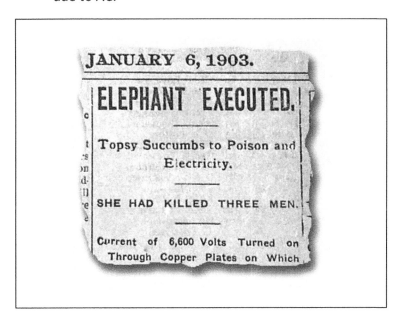

Slide 8 (MIDDLE):

But AC is not less safe than DC, and in many cases safer than DC, since it's not direct current at the required voltage. While landlines are going away as time goes on, the reason why you don't get electrocuted when picking up a landline telephone during lightning and an electrical storm, is due to AC. And I think we'd all agree, this is a good thing.

Slide 9 (MIDDLE):

However, DC makes a lot of sense for a variety of applications when you don't need electricity traveling for long distances. Battery chargers are just one of many examples.

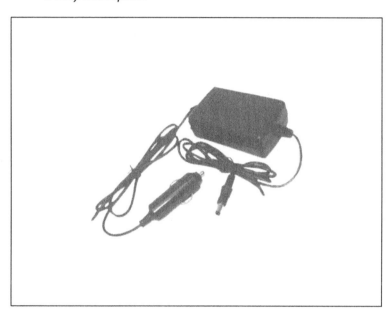

Slide 10 (TRANSITION TO END):

These two men, once friends and partners and eventually bitter foes, were both brilliant for their contributions and wound up sharing the Nobel Prize.

Slide 11 (END):

Truth be told, while all passionate people, driven to success by personal ambition and a desire to change the world may have conflicting world views, the world would not be the same if it were NOT for the important contributions of both Edison and Tesla. And AC and DC power, as we know it, may not have existed.

So as I mentioned, there are many ways to put a presentation together and this is just one, small example, this should give you an indication of how to generally organize and structure your presentation.

CHAPTER THREE |
LEARNING FROM
COMEDIANS

I use comedians as a tool when I teach business communications. Specifically, I use stand-up comedians because I believe we stand to learn a lot about <u>audiences</u> by observing successful comedians.

When you think about your favorite comedian, you probably like them more for their style rather than their jokes, I'll guess. In other words, the content — the joke — is usually secondary. It's the **delivery** of the joke that makes you laugh.

Ever hear a really great friend of yours who you really like and care about but isn't funny ruin a completely great joke? The joke is a great one. But the "wrong" person is telling the joke. So, the content is secondary. The delivery is what gives it a great punch line.

There are probably only a few things worse than a person who's trying to be funny but isn't funny.

Aside from understanding your content when delivering a presentation, you also have to determine *how to connect* with your audience.

Comedians have an instinctual understanding of their audiences. They need to. It's a survival skill; it's how they eat! George Carlin, Richard Pryor, Chris Rock, Dave Chappelle, etc. Your favorite comedian, whomever they are, living or not, were once starving artists – literally and figuratively.

Stand-up comedians have an ability – and opportunity and necessity, in some cases – that even the most famous actors don't. Since comedians have to be so in-tuned with their audience, it's one of the only, if not *the* only, theatrical art form where the comedian (presenter) has the opportunity to adjust their style, pitch, tone, etc. in real time, as needed, based on their read of the audience. That's pretty amazing.

Good comedians (and I mean the really good ones, if you're a genuine fan of comedy) will not go after tepid laughter. Maybe that's how they started their careers. But every good (great) comedian I have observed/studied will do away with the tepid laughter that may resonate "a little" with a general audience.

Instead, they'll take RISKS and go after the big laughs once they understand their audience – their core base. And of course, their audience will also understand them.

Comedians also need to have lots of courage to say what they want to say. Otherwise, there is no point.

In preparing for your next presentation, watch your favorite comedian on YouTube and see what it is, as far as a "total package," makes you laugh. I'm ready to bet that more of it rests on the delivery. If you don't have a favorite, can I make a suggestion? Watch George Carlin.

When you watch Carlin on stage, observe what he's doing. Observe his body language, and how he masters the skill of connecting with his audience while remembering his lines. He was a true artist.

CHAPTER FOUR | AUDIENCE AND SELF-AWARENESS

Two of the key issues regarding effective presentations include the ability to understand your audience and self-awareness.

Before I go into detail, the biggest piece of practical advice I can give you here is to make sure you *never* alienate your audience. Always remember that within the context of a presentation, you are not the focus; they are. You work for them, in that moment. You really do. The extent of your knowledge is not relevant. If you're successful, you'll get the credit you deserve. What you can give your audience matters, and that will make all the difference. This can be tricky, because even if you're a polished speaker and you forget your audience, you'll fail. I guarantee this.

For instance:

- What is the purpose of being an expert on something if your audience doesn't absorb the info you want them to?
- What is the point of trying to give advice to a room full of people that won't be able to use it?
- What is the purpose of being a marketing maven if you wind up making your presentation pretty much all about yourself and no one in the audience takes away anything from your message?

SELF-AWARENESS

Being self-aware means that you have a strong sense of your surroundings, what you can reasonably understand about your audience, and most importantly – what you can reasonably assume they know about you.

To focus on the last point, your title isn't as important as you think when you're addressing an audience. Whether you're a CEO, Director, head coach, politician, teacher, etc., your credibility is only as good as what people think of you. As you know, perception is reality.

If you have good credibility, great. If you don't have good credibility but also aren't self-aware of your situation, you'll most likely have a presentation or speech that fails.

If you're suffering from low credibility (for whatever) reason, you can still deliver a great presentation. Just be honest about things. You know the phrase "the elephant in the room," so address the elephant.

I find that if you're candid about what you think the audience thinks (about you or a situation), your credibility immediately shoots up. You've addressed the audience's concern, and they can now relax a little bit – and actually listen to what you have to say.

Believe me when I tell you that I've seen the following so many times at the professional and industry level.

A few years ago, I was excited to go to a presentation by a very well-known and respected person in my industry. Of course, I won't share her name but know that she's a leader in the beauty industry. The presentation was meant to be about how she started her business empire, and the event was marketed as an entrepreneurship/innovation talk.

I hate to tell you how disappointed I was. All she did was talk about herself. Ninety-five percent of her presentation was an autobiography in disguise. I got nothing out of the evening. I didn't learn. I wasn't inspired. I wasn't entertained. Nothing. Oh wait, there was free pizza. Correction, I got a slice of pizza. My apologies.

In most, if not all cases, when you do a presentation, **make it about them (the audience), not you.** Ask yourself this simple question: What can my audience get out of this? People not only love to talk about themselves but also love to hear about themselves. We love attention.

At one point I worked for a prominent company, one that I still have great admiration for. I remember attending a presentation by a division president who came from the outside with a bit of cache behind his name. He started the presentation by saying "I'm going to talk about my favorite topic...me." I don't think he was joking; he was being serious. How do you think the audience reacted? Stoned faces and silence. He then got a little awkward, but he probably deserved it.

So make it about the audience, not you!

Let me share a basic example of how you can tailor things to an audience, to give you a sense:

Let's say you're doing a presentation on how injected plastic products are manufactured.

If you're sharing info to a specific audience, such as a class of technical students, you may say something like this (from Wikipedia):

Injection molding is a manufacturing process for producing parts by injecting molten material into a mold. Injection molding can be performed with a host of materials, often polymers. Material for the part is fed into a heated barrel, mixed (using a helical shaped screw), and injected (forced) into a mold cavity, where it cools and hardens to the configuration of the cavity.

Now let's say you're doing a presentation to a general audience about the same thing. You may want to try something like this (I have a background in injection molding so this is my own interpretation):

So, ever wonder how the plastic parts that you use every day are made? Anything from a typical pen, to your remote control, the dashboard in a car, etc., etc.?

Plastic starts its life as resin pellets; small little round balls. This resin is poured into a hopper where it gets very hot and semi-melted. From there, it oozes into what's called a mold, which is the shape of the actual product – in two mirror-image parts. As the hot resin squeezes into the mold, the mold closes with an intense amount of pressure – remains closed from anywhere from 5 seconds to a few minutes (depending on the size and shape of the product) and then releases. The product then immediately begins to cool and falls into an exit chute. And voila! There's the outer casing for your remote control.

I think this is suitable for a general audience, as an intro. And I think it makes the point in an easier way, and you get more out of it this way.

- I provided some context to bring it to life with some product examples that most of us are familiar with.
- I tried to simplify the process without using too much jargon.

51

- I tried to use some descriptive language instead to offer relatability – "oozes." I wouldn't use that term in my industry, but I think it works here.
- I mentioned that the mold stays closed for a certain amount of time – which is what we technically call "cycle time." But I didn't use that term. No need to.
- I didn't offer many details, such as the types of resin available (there are so many types of resins, btw). And I didn't get into colors, etc.

CASUAL INTRODUCTIONS

While there is a dedicated chapter on introductions and different intro techniques, I'd like to talk a little about casual introductions here. But remember that this is here in this chapter as it relates to the importance of your audience.

What I mean by a casual introduction is taking the opportunity to "break the ice" with your audience. It's the verbal equivalent of shaking hands. It's a pre-introduction, in other words, prior to jumping into your actual presentation and your actual introduction technique.

Let me share with you a technique I borrowed from politicians on both sides of the aisle. It works more with audiences that you don't know.

I first need to tell you two unofficial terms I came up with: "guaranteed" and "non-guaranteed" audiences.

Non-guaranteed audiences are audiences that don't have to be there. So you need to work hard not only to keep them, but to "hook" them from the start.

Guaranteed audiences are your employees, whether you're a CEO, SVP, VP, or department head of some type. They can also be your cohorts in a classroom setting, etc. Guaranteed audiences are essentially audiences that will be there whether they want to or not, to put it simply.

Non-guaranteed audiences are clearly harder. Here are some examples of where you may find non-guaranteed audiences:

- Sales presentations
- Fundraising meetings
- Union meetings
- Political stump speeches

One way to capture the attention of a non-guaranteed audience is to tell them what you think they want to hear, starting with your introduction. I realize that doesn't sound so good to everyone but let me explain with a personal anecdote.

About two years ago, I was asked to do a presentation on marketing/entrepreneurship to a group of veterans at an institution that I've been associated with for a very long time. It's a program that offers veterans an opportunity to go into business for themselves. The program doesn't have traditional grades or rigid attendance, and those in the program are not really considered students. So I knew that while my presentation was part of the overall program, the participants didn't necessarily have to be there the entire time.

I've done hundreds of presentations, but admittedly I stressed over this one beforehand, not because of the content I was going to share – I knew my stuff— but because of how I felt I needed to start. I wanted to acknowledge their service in the armed forces while at the same time not coming off as disingenuous.

I finally decided to muster up enough courage and introduce the presentation like this:

Before we begin, I just want to quickly thank you all for your service and sacrifice.

Judging from the warm smiles that I saw across the room of approximately 30 veterans, I knew it was a big hit. It takes some nerve to do it, *believe me*, but this *actually* works.

If you're a businessperson and you're rallying students around a cause that you're a big benefactor to, for example, you may want to say something like (I'll use New York University, since that's one of my alma maters):

Isn't it a great day to be a Violet!?

In that case, you wait for an applause. And unless you're a very controversial figure, I don't see why you wouldn't get a big one. Remember, **this technique is about praising them.**

If you're worried about not getting an applause, just ask for one (and start applauding too, off course). Just slightly adjust and say this:

Isn't it a great day to be a Violet!? Why don't you all give yourselves a round of applause, you deserve it!

I have to seriously say I think this is so much better than talking about the weather, assuming the weather is nice. The president of a company once started a presentation talking about the weather for an entire two minutes. It was mid-September and there was about two weeks of no rain and that slightly cooler, but still nice September weather (tristate area).   Seriously, two minutes is a long time to talk about the weather! I was honestly saying to myself, "Ok dude, I get it, it's nice outside."

Another thing you may want to try, before getting into the actual introduction to your presentation, is to compliment the audience on a basic level. Since I'm also an adjunct instructor, there has been times in my career where I spoke to incoming interns on behalf of the company I was working for. On those occasions, I used the following type of casual introductions:

So great to meet you all. Thanks so much for coming in on a Friday morning in the middle of the summer. Don't worry, I won't talk too long and get in the way of your weekend plans.

If you're concerned, no, this isn't an example of not being confident or being concerned with taking up their time. This is simply being a little political (in a good way) and starting the process of connecting with them. It also shows that, once again, you are self-aware. It works a little better than just rhetorically asking "How are you?" I'm sure the incoming interns are excited about working in your company in the Fall, but they are most likely 18-21-year-olds, and YES, in the middle of the summer on a Friday they probably have the beach or weekend plans on their minds!

Remember that whether you are a CEO, a student, or anything in between, when you're giving a presentation, you're working for the audience.

DON'T (NECESSARILY) ASSUME

I'll keep this short and sweet. Let's say you're doing a presentation on an individual. Don't necessarily assume that everyone in the room knows your subject. If you can safely assume and you definitively know that they know, fine. But even with famous people, don't assume. I think it's hard to find anyone above the age of, say, 15 or so, that doesn't know who Socrates was. But you should make a quick reference of some kind, especially if you're not certain that everyone knows your subject. Also, if you have a photo of Socrates on a slide, you should provide some reference to him. Most people don't know what Socrates looked like as a man.

Remembering your audience means the <u>Who, What, and Why</u>, and they're intermingled.

THE WHO

For example, if you're a heart surgeon and doing a presentation on the latest techniques in heart transplant surgery, you'll adjust depending on whether you're speaking to a room of your peers such as other heart surgeons at a conference or speaking to a room of medical students.

If it's to a group of medical students, you may need to provide some base info that you wouldn't need to provide to a group of heart surgeons.

CONNECT THE DOTS

Caution here...don't fall into a classic trap! As in the above scenario, there will be times when you'll need to provide some base info, not because the audience may not know it—they may— but because they may need to be presented with it in order to connect one thing to another. The heart surgeons already know how to connect things without you explicitly saying it. In this case, providing the base information to the medical students serves as reinforcement or a reminder rather than "teaching" it to them.

THE WHAT

Let's say you're an investment whiz and have made millions trading in the market. It's important to you to help the layperson learn some of the techniques that made you successful.

If you're doing a presentation to a group of middle-class, first-time investors, you'll want to not only simplify the information, but also tone down your rhetoric. Rhetoric doesn't always have to be a bad thing. But if you're an investment whiz, let's face it, you've probably gained a wealth of experience and with that comes a level of confidence and an "air" of being pretty sure of yourself. That style might be completely fine with your peers, but won't work all that well with first-time investors. They have no use for the "bravado;" they need the building blocks. Also, you want to ensure you're not intimidating them.

THE WHY

Your objective may not be as obvious to your audience as you may think. When Steve Jobs introduced the iPad in 2010 during one of his famous Apple keynotes, the audience had a good idea of what he was going to share. For months there had been news and rumors in the tech world about Apple introducing a tablet.

What Jobs decided to do was to start off by discussing the iPhone and Mac. You may think that was irrelevant for introducing a new tablet, but he chose to walk us through what the phone and the laptop did and didn't do as well, so he could set the stage for a third-category device that would be better for certain tasks. Jobs keenly understood that his work on the iPad wasn't complete; he still needed to communicate the value proposition to the skeptics and walk us through why we should carry around a third device.

Hindsight is always 20/20. In retrospect, that was a smart move in his presentation technique. If he started with the iPad and its functions, some members of the audience still wouldn't know why we needed it. The take away here is just because your audience may know the what, you still need to tell them the why. That's *your* job, not theirs.

CHAPTER FIVE | OBJECTIVE

As mentioned earlier, you will want to establish what your overall objective is when preparing your presentation. In simple terms, always ask yourself what is it that you're trying to *achieve.* While this may seem a bit obvious, it's sometimes taken for granted.

Are you trying to share some information with an audience? If so, it is probably more than an FYI. If it *is* just a simple FYI, and you'd rather discuss it rather than sending an email, then we probably don't even need to call those situations "presentations."

If you're sharing information, such as an update, are you also trying to persuade? You may not be selling them, per se, but are you trying to influence some type of behavior i.e. offering an alternative insurance plan or unveiling a new business strategy that requires employees to embrace a new mindset? Alternatively, are you doing a highly interactive type of presentation that requires high audience involvement?

SHOW AND TELL

Remember when you were a kid and had "show and tell" in school? Those were exciting – and also simpler – times, for sure. And I'm assuming that your kindergarten or first-grade teacher didn't grill you on your objective when you came to show and tell, right?

But if you really think about it, even the simple, innocent activity of show and tell can begin to teach us how we should think of presentations, as adults.

I'm sure you either brought something into class to discuss? Maybe it was a new doll that you were excited about. Maybe you didn't have a toy to bring but you brought pictures from a family vacation and you told all of your cute, little classmates about it? Maybe you got a new puppy and while you couldn't bring Fido to school, you decided to tell the students why you got a dog instead of a cat, because of your allergies, etc.

Anyway, the innocence of kids, coupled with show and tell and all of its unassuming objectives can give us a pretty good starting point to think about your presentation.

THE FOUR OBJECTIVES

There are generally four main objectives of a presentation (many authors will use different names), but they essentially boil down to the same four. And they are not always fixed-point. In other words, sometimes you can do a presentation that has a bit of a blend of two or more.

For example, if you're a coach giving your players a locker room pep talk on what they need to do to win, don't necessarily assume this is a tell/sell situation just because you're the coach and the players are your subordinates. This could be both tell/sell and consult/join, since a good coach knows that he needs the support from the players (the audience) in order to carry out the mission. Lecturing players simply isn't going to cut it. I use Al Pacino's "locker room" speech from *Any Given Sunday* to illustrate this (see appendix B).

Borrowing a page from Mary Munter and Lynn Hamilton, the objective of a presentation can be thought of as one of the following:

- Tell/Sell – used primarily when you want the audience to learn from you.
- Consult/Join – used primarily when you want to learn from the audience, or need buy-in.

You can categorize them in many ways, such as:

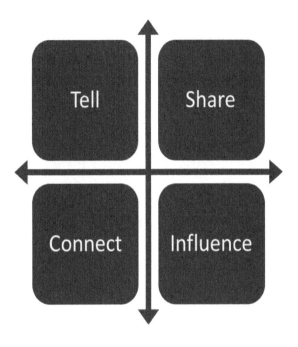

Let's map this out a little more specifically so you can get a better appreciation of what skills and attributes go with these, and hopefully you'll get a better handle on how to prepare your presentation.

	Skills	Attributes
Tell	Present Simplify Summarize Interpret	Clarity Precision Discipline Confidence Tenacity
Connect	Listen Question Discuss Probe Debate Provide/Receive Feedback	Openness Candor Patience Curiosity Humility Accessibility
Share	Engage Collaborate Facilitate Navigate	Respect Trust Empathy Self-awareness
Influence	Propose Persuade Lead	Transparency Authenticity/Passion Decisiveness

Another important issue when forming your objective is to ensure your presentation isn't too broad. We'll discuss agendas in another chapter but, as you begin to structure your presentation based on what you hope to achieve, make sure the various components are not so general that they become separate presentations in of themselves.

In other words, try not to do too much and be overly ambitious. Presentations and speeches can land you a promotion, a new job, a new account. Heck, a solid presentation/speech sometimes changes the world in some way (see Nelson Mandela). However, they are specific in terms of their objective. People who understand strategy know that by staying focused, they stay relevant.

PLAN, BUT WITH A LITTLE FLEXIBILITY

If you plan *too* "well" in advance, you may come across as too scripted and inauthentic, so avoid doing this. You don't want to be perceived as a "cookie cutter" or "plain vanilla" speaker. Plan well but leave in a little "wiggle room." It is understandable if in your line of work you mainly deliver tell/sell presentations that are generally straightforward. Add your own flair and dynamic, though, and make something that might be boring a little *less* boring. If you plan well but are perceived as "militant" about it, you'll quickly gain the reputation being a boring and rigid presenter.

We all know what happens when you grab a handful of sand too tightly. It slides through your fingers. If you hold it too loosely, it falls from the sides of your hands. Hold it just right, with a little firmness, and most of the sand can stay in your hand.

LEVEL OF DETAILS

The most important thing here is to make sure you don't confuse detail with simplification. To the extent you can, be sure to simplify when and where it makes sense. Simplification is universally good, since it means you're making your content easy to digest.

The amount of details you provide partly has to do with your depth of knowledge of the subject. And as you hopefully guessed by now, after reading everything I said about audiences – it's also about your audience.

When I took business communications during my MBA studies, the instructor mentioned that good/the best presenters have a strong command of details. That's good advice, but I've changed my opinion about that advice over the years. It doesn't necessarily mean that you need to share all of the details. Keep that in mind.

Knowing the amount of details to provide can be tricky but understanding your audience and your objective should make this a lot less daunting. I touched on this above with the example on heart surgeons but let's expand a bit more.

We have a tendency, especially when we're passionate about our subject, to give far too much detail than necessary. It's a natural inclination, and I think we do it for the following reasons:

1. We're presenting to a group of superiors and we feel that we are proving our value by showcasing our command of the details.

Most of us, myself included, have been in this situation. Have some faith in your superiors and don't overcompensate. They themselves were once in your position, but even if they weren't, they trust you. Don't waste their time. If they need more detail, they will ask.

2. We think we need to demonstrate how we reached a conclusion.

This is different than connecting the dots, as I mentioned with the previous heart surgeon example. Here, we feel as though we need to justify our conclusions, approach, recommendations, etc. by offering the logic or sequence of events that got us there. You don't always need to. In business, we primarily care about results!

3. We assume that since *we* care so much about the subject matter, our *audience* also does.

This is a classic mistake. Sorry to say this, but even people who are interested in the presentation simply may not care as much about the subject as we do. I know this can be a bit disconcerting because we want people to care. But it's better that this come from me rather than being unsuccessful with your presentation and then *really* being upset.

4.   We are barking up the wrong tree.

This is mainly a function of having the right message but delivering it to the wrong audience. You may have heard the saying, "you're preaching to the choir." This is similar, in the sense that you're giving excessive details to people who don't need them.

So how do we know what is the right amount of details?

My best advice is think about when you should *stop*. In other words, consider when you've made your point to your particular audience. At what point do you no longer need to share additional information to support each major idea? Stop there. Another way to approach this is to ask yourself, "at what point does the amount of detail I share stop adding value to the audience?"

Providing too many details can have the reverse effect of what you hoped for. I have a lot of respect for R&D people and have worked with them and other technical people throughout my career. But sometimes technical people make the mistake of offering too much detail to non-technical audiences. In those cases, it's not only that the amount of details offered is unnecessary, but there's a good chance the audience, often merchants and marketing people, won't understand it. So be mindful of this.

Think for a moment about a recent vacation you went on. You've returned and are telling your friends and co-workers about your trip. You may give certain friends more detail than co-workers, but you'll still leave out the things that have no bearing on anything, right?

Having a time limit for your presentation can also help keep you guided.

Here's an example:

You're doing a presentation to a general audience on the 4-stroke engine, commonly known as the gasoline-powered engine. This engine, created and patented by Karl Benz in 1886, is still used in most cars today. A four-stroke, or four-cycle, engine is an internal combustion (IC) engine in which the piston completes four separate strokes while turning the crankshaft.

Look at the difference between the original and condensed version.

The four separate strokes are termed (original version from Wikipedia):

ORIGINAL: 1.Intake: also known as induction or suction. This stroke of the piston begins at top dead center (T.D.C.) and ends at bottom dead center (B.D.C.). In this stroke, the intake valve must be in the open position while the piston pulls an air-fuel mixture into the cylinder by producing vacuum pressure into the cylinder through its downward motion. The piston is moving down as air is being sucked in by the downward motion against the piston.

CONDENSED: 1.Intake: This stroke of the piston begins at the top and ends at the bottom. The piston is moving down as air is being sucked in.

ORIGINAL: 2.Compression: This stroke begins at B.D.C, or just at the end of the suction stroke, and ends at T.D.C. In this stroke, the piston compresses the air-fuel mixture in preparation for ignition during the power stroke (below). Both the intake and exhaust valves are closed during this stage.

CONDENSED: 2.Compression: The piston compresses the air-fuel mixture in preparation for ignition. Both the intake and exhaust valves are closed.

ORIGINAL: 3.Combustion: also known as power or ignition This is the start of the second revolution of the four-stroke cycle. At this point the crankshaft has completed a full 360-degree revolution. While the piston is at T.D.C. (the end of the compression stroke) the compressed air-fuel mixture is ignited by a spark plug (in a gasoline engine) or by heat generated by high compression (diesel engines), forcefully returning the piston to B.D.C. This stroke produces mechanical work from the engine to turn the crankshaft.

CONDENSED: 3.Combustion: also known as ignition. The compressed air-fuel mixture is ignited by a spark plug (in a gasoline engine) or by heat generated by high compression (diesel engines).

ORIGINAL: 4.Exhaust: also known as outlet. During the *exhaust* stroke, the piston once again returns from B.D.C. to T.D.C. while the exhaust valve is open. This action expels the spent air-fuel mixture through the exhaust valve.

CONDENSED: 4.Exhaust: During the *exhaust* stroke, the piston once again returns from the bottom to the top while the exhaust valve is open. This action expels the spent air-fuel mixture through the exhaust valve.

Hopefully you notice that in the condensed version, the nature of the information hasn't changed. I just reduced the *amount* of information.

Another red flag that you might be offering too much detail is if your presentation's topic fundamentally changes at some point during your delivery – literally.

I once observed a presentation that had a lot of great elements to it in the beginning but quickly derailed. The topic was on immigration and the presentation started out very strong. The presenter began by discussing the crisis in Syria – but soon enough the presentation shifted from immigration to the Syrian war.

It wasn't intentional, but the entire presentation changed because the presenter got wrapped up in too many details on the war.

CHAPTER SIX | OWNING YOUR CONTENT

I've probably seen thousands of presentations over the years given by industry colleagues and my own students. One thing I would immediately notice is whether the presenters truly owned their content. When I say owning content I don't mean memorization. In almost all cases, memorization is the *opposite* of ownership.

Ownership has to do with being comfortable with the content to the extent that you understand it. That doesn't mean you need to be an expert on the entire subject. But it *does* mean that you need to be an "expert" as far as the content of the presentation is concerned.

However, while this may seem contradictory, if you truly don't understand all aspects of your content, sometimes the *perception of* owning your content can be just as good or good enough. I'm not encouraging you to *not* learn your content, but I'm being realistic. I'm sure you've heard this before – perception is reality.

When you own your content, you speak to it with confidence. People command the room when they own their content, and this directly correlates with your confidence.

I've seen introverts turn into extroverts when they deliver an excellent speech and own their content. I once had an introverted student who needed some improvement. He did an exceptional job on the final presentation of the semester. It came alive. He gave a presentation on day trading and shared that he was a day trader. He owned his content. He had a command of the ideas and words coming out of his mouth. He had a great time presenting, and his confidence was at an all-time high.

One of my best friends, who I've known since elementary school, is the most confident person I've ever met. He's a former high school and college track star and is currently an actor and high school teacher. Will he ever become the next Al Pacino or Matt Damon? It's likely that will never happen. But no matter what he does, act or teach, his confidence is his greatest asset. It's not BS; it lives within the core of his chest and pours out in whatever he does. Everyone sees it.

OWNERSHIP VS. MEMORIZATION

Ownership doesn't mean memorization. If you truly feel the need to memorize, and you can do it without coming across as robotic, go for it. Steve Jobs did this, for the most part, when he delivered his famed Apple Keynotes throughout the years. But I can tell you, as a marketing and innovation guy, Jobs was the exception in many ways. Most of us are not like him.

There's one other exception—actors and performers. However, they are trained on how to come across as natural. It's part of their craft and is expected of them. That's why they call it acting.

But most of us, including myself, are mere mortals. If you try to memorize you'll most likely come across as robotic. Believe me when I tell you that your audience will be able tell. Your eyes will have a blank stare, and you'll have an unnatural look on your face as if you're processing data. Why? Well, because you are.

The other problem with memorization is that if you miss a word, that may completely ruin your presentation. One missed word can generally throw everything out of sequence. So don't work so hard if you don't have to. Or, work hard towards other aspects of your presentation. Actors need to memorize their scripts. You and I do not.

In the next chapter, we'll discuss ways that will complement how to own your content and come across as authentic.

CHAPTER SEVEN | YOUR STYLE

This chapter is devoted to the qualities/characteristics that will ultimately make you the type of presenter want to be. While there isn't only one right way to present, these guidelines will help become effective in shaping your unique style.

PERSONALITY

Your genuine personality will also be reflective of your presentations. You can't escape it, and there is no need to. Be comfortable in your own skin.

Presenting takes practice in terms of strategy and execution, but you also want to make sure that you are yourself when you present. Whatever your personality is, make it work for you, so you can engage with your audience.

If you're a funny person, great! Run with it. Tell a joke in the beginning, during or at the end of your presentation.

I'm not a funny person. I just don't have that quality, but I do have others. On occasion when I *am* funny, I'm funny by accident. At least that's what my friends would say. So, I avoid *trying* to be funny whenever I present or teach. I'd be a big failure otherwise.

Sometimes I can be funny by being self-deprecating (which I love doing) and that may apply to you too. But I focus on my personality traits instead; being sincere and a straight shooter.

So, I don't believe in the advice that many communications books offer – be funny or tell a joke in your presentations. How can you be funny if you're not funny? You can't.

Funny people are born, not made, for the most part. You know all of those comedians that you have never heard of that you've also never seen on Saturday Night Live and for some reason you keep missing their HBO comedy specials? Oh, that's right, because those were the comedians that failed because they weren't funny. You can go to business school, medical school, dental school, bartender school, cosmetology school, and you can even go for improv lessons, etc. But last time I checked, there isn't a "Funny School."

Whether you're funny, serious, or sincere – just make sure you're *authentic*. When you're trying to be something you're not, your audience *will* notice. In fact, strangers will be able to detect this even faster and more intuitively than your friends and co-workers. It's a law of nature.

BODY LANGUAGE

Many books on communications will offer a significant amount of techniques when it comes to body language. For example, some presentation coaches will tell you to never place your hands in your pockets. Others say it's fine. Some books offer advice on your shoulders being parallel to your feet. The list goes on. While I respect some of the advice, I don't use all of it and have never quite believed in them *too much.* Many of those tid-bits of advice just seem so technical. Furthermore, they are not necessary for a successful presentation. Nonetheless, and not to sound like a hypocrite, I am providing the most important things I've learned over the years.

Body language is indeed *incredibly* important. But the best advice I can give is to be natural. Be comfortable in your own skin. This takes practice for some of us and comes a bit easier for the rest of us. And again, when you *own* your content, you feel comfortable. You have full command of the room. Here are some general take-aways on body language:

- I tend to walk around the room a bit. Obviously, this also depends a bit on the logistics of the room. Just make sure it's not arbitrary. If done properly, this can be very purposeful. Walking around the room at times keeps people's eyes on you and it literally keeps the air in the room flowing and fresh. In a larger room, it also gives your audience the feeling that you're giving all sides of the room attention.

- While there may be times when you have no choice but to speak behind a podium, my advice is to avoid them. Don't *hide* behind podiums! Show yourself. With some exceptions, podiums are for those who don't like to speak.
- While I don't put much emphasis on whether you have your shoulders parallel to your feet, etc., I've noticed that some men tend to have their feet glued to the floor and they end up rocking their bodies back-and-forth. I've never understood that, so just please avoid it.
- To be an equal opportunity critic for a moment, I sometimes see women cross their feet. This can be a sign of nervousness or taking the presentation too casually. Please also be mindful of this and try your best to avoid it.
- Make sure that you don't have any "lazy" head movements. I've seen head movements that just don't coincide with anything. People notice that sort of thing, believe me.

You want to create a balance between running the presentation and *physically* connecting with your audience.

It's also worth mentioning how crucial your physical proximity to your audience is. I've seen many presenters stand near the wall and away from their audience. I don't believe this in intentional, but it does send the wrong message. Even if you don't walk around the room and choose to stay stationary, try not to be physically distant. You don't want to breathe down people's throats, but at the same time don't be shy. Get a little close. Show some warmth.

FACIAL EXPRESSIONS AND MISCONSTRUED INTENT

Facial expressions are clearly important. But I think there's something about them that needs to be addressed. I've seen some presentations over the years where the intro was meant to be fairly straightforward, but the audience began laughing. In a case like that, I'm critical of the presenter. If it was meant to be straightforward, then they didn't do enough to keep it straightforward. If it was, indeed, meant as a joke and the audience started laughing, well the presenter "got away" with their poor facial expressions and the audience gave them a freebie. They got lucky on that one.

So make sure that you can control your facial expressions and they relate back to your intent. If there's something poignant you are sharing at one point in your presentation, for example, don't be afraid to open your eyes wider than usual – or whatever the occasion may call for.

THE POWER OF A SMILE

Don't underestimate the power of a smile. If you're doing a presentation that doesn't call for a smile, whether because of a hostile audience, a sad situation, etc., then obviously don't. In general, though, a smile can go a long way. Granted women might be naturally a bit better at this than men. When a presenter smiles, it causes audience members to smile and that's powerful.

Have you ever noticed that when you're walking down the street by yourself, thinking of something positive and you are naturally smiling, strangers passing in the other direction will give you a smile or partial smile back? You're radiating positive energy. If it works on the street with strangers, trust me, it will also work in a controlled environment like during presentation or speech.

EYE CONTACT

While also overstated, effective eye contact is a prerequisite for effective presentations. Poor eye contact can sometimes indicate either a lack of confidence or lack of interest. Over the years I've noticed and categorized three general patterns:

Good eye contact

People with good eye contact have the ability to look at others while they're speaking, even when it speaking to crowds of people. When you give your audience good eye contact, you are "in the moment," truly connecting your eyes with your audience as you deliver your presentation. The key is to provide as equal of an amount of your eye contact to the entire audience, to the extent that it makes sense, of course.

Limited eye contact

Limited eye contact means that people are utilizing effective eye contact techniques, but only for a small range of their audience. For example, in a room of 20 people, they might be providing good eye contact to only about 3 or 4 (25 percent). This is quite common. Perhaps you're in eye contact of those you trust or find pleasing. You'll need to practice not relying on that all of the time and be more democratic.

No (or poor) eye contact

This one is obvious. People with no eye contact do two things— essentially, they either look at the floor the entire time or look/read from their slides. At times, poor eye contact may appear to be eye contact when it really isn't. This occurs when people stare blankly, essentially looking at nothing or looking "through" the audience. Don't look through people, look *at* them.

Another sign of poor eye contact is when the speaker attempts to look at the audience but instead he/she looks at the adjacent wall at about eye level. By looking at the adjacent wall, they are essentially looking at nothing.

IMPROVING EYE CONTACT

I'll be honest, there's no overnight solution for those with poor eye contact, but it's fixable with the right techniques. There are several things you want to first figure out about yourself before you can identify exactly what needs improvement in your presentations.

Are you the type who walks down the halls of your company and puts your head down when someone you don't know walks by? You have to be honest with yourself. If so, you may have a general lack of confidence. That's most likely a larger issue than just presenting and outside the scope of this guide. What about when you watch someone else speak? Do you get uncomfortable when someone with good eye contact makes eye contact with you?

If you don't get uncomfortable when others speak and make eye contact with you, that's a good start. Perhaps you're concerned with how long you make eye contact with them. Your poor eye contact might stem from a fear that it may come across as though you're staring, or maybe even creepy? If the length of time is what is holding you back, look at their eyes for a few seconds before you look at another part of their face and then go back to their eyes, etc.

You don't have to "gaze" into someone's eyes in some type of romantic way to provide good eye contact. In other words, you don't have to be intense about it as though you're trying to profess your love for them. Remember, you're not staring, you're looking. You don't have to look directly into someone's pupils if you're not comfortable. Instead, you can look around and near their eyes before you get more comfortable.

If you've practiced this and are now more comfortable on an individual level, things should get easier for presentations. You want to provide equal amount of eye contact with everyone, especially for smaller audiences of 40 or less. Some people may tell you to practice by making a pattern in your mind, like a "Figure 8." Do this only if you really need it. But I wouldn't recommend this for two reasons:

1. It seems like that would take more brain power than it should; brain power that can be used elsewhere for better purposes.

2. If you're truly doing a pattern, do you really want to be doing a "continuous loop," like a robot?

While presenting to large audiences, actual eye contact will probably only happen with certain people in the audience. You'll still want to divide the room up, in thirds or quadrants, and practice the concept of giving each section approximately equal amounts of eye contact.

I'm calling what I do the "dart board" approach. (And I sincerely hope this isn't some type of well-known approach that someone will say I'm taking credit for). But with this approach, what I generally do is look at my overall audience as a dart board. Depending on the logistics of the room and how my audience is "shaped" – round, oval, U-shaped, rectangular, like a baseball stadium, etc., I point my eyes at various areas of my audience. And no, I'm not just trying to hit the bullseye. I'm darting my eyes around naturally. Hopefully how a typical dart player would play darts...the darts will fall naturally around the board.

Once you begin to get better at this, I think ultimately the best eye contact should be natural. If you're sitting in the audience, wouldn't you want the presenter to give you some of their attention from time-to-time via eye contact? I think most people would say yes.

As I previously said, when you're giving a presentation you're working for the audience. You have to work!

YOUR "POKER" FACE

Whether in a corporate or classroom setting, I can guarantee your audience is not going to be made up of equally-attentive listeners. That's just a fact. In any audience, whether we know them or not, we have people who will give us more of their attention, give us consistent eye contact, tune in to what we're saying, etc. We will also have audience members whose negative body language suggests that they don't care or are indifferent. They may be distracted, not even looking, etc.

I know what you're thinking: Not only is it disheartening when we are up in front of an audience giving an important talk and we don't receive the attention we feel we deserve, but we may have a natural tendency to ignore them too. Unfortunately, you can't do that. Let's be realistic.

The audience members that give you positive attentiveness are the ones who you'll probably make more eye contact with and be in close physical proximity. However, you can't ignore the less attentive ones. You have to create a "poker face" and, while you may not be thrilled—and believe me, this has happened to me in both corporate and classroom situations— you will still need to give them eye contact and some of your positive body language as well.

Whenever you're in a speaking position, you're in a leadership position. That's on you. If they still don't respond, at least you did your part. Honestly, though, if your presentation is long enough (a few hours in total, etc.), you have a chance of winning over some of those inattentive audience members.

IT'S NOT ALWAYS ABOUT YOU

Sometimes audience members who appear inattentive and as though they don't care may be having a bad day or may be distracted for completely different reason unrelated to you. Perhaps they have a headache; maybe they just got off the subway in the middle of a July heatwave and need a few minutes to cool off. It's even possible that their natural disposition causes them to appear withdrawn, but they are actually listening intently.

Therefore, you want to be aware of those audience members but not jump to any premature conclusions. If you write them off by ignoring them, then they may truly be turned off. So, don't read too much into it. Be a little patient and, more importantly, be a leader. Not always, but sometimes, you'll be pleasantly surprised at the outcome.

INFLECTION, TONE, PITCH

Being monotone is a universally bad thing. I'm sure you've heard this. Speaking in a monotone way means that there is no pitch variety. Everything you say sounds the same. Have you ever known someone to suffer from the following issues?

- They're trying to be sarcastic, but it comes across as serious?
- They have something exciting and positive to say but it's tough for them to convince you that they are excited?
- They have some bad news to share but they don't seem upset?
- They always sound tired when they speak?

Honestly, I'm don't want to be harsh, but no one wants to listen to a monotone speaker. There should be a natural element to adjusting your pitch as you

speak. Sometimes we need to exaggerate a little.
Sometimes A LOT! Sometimes we need to
remember to emote. Our voice should have rhythm
to it and you need to allow it to go up and down as
needed.

The good news is that I simply don't believe that
people who are monotone can't do anything about
it. If you were to take each monotone speaker and
observe them in their personal lives, or at least in a
non-presenting capacity, I bet you would see them in
a different light. I would bet money that they are not
monotone.

It might be easier than you think to help improve this
if you've been accused of being monotone.
Remember there are really only three ways your
voice can go. Up, down, or level. All three are
necessary. But you need to practice when to use
them in harmony.

Consider this: Would you necessarily say the
following sentences in the same exact way?

- *Tomorrow is garbage day. Make sure to leave
the garbage curbside.*
- *I just got an offer for my dream job. I've been
interviewing with that company for months and I
finally got it.*

I would hope that you'd have more expression in
your voice with respect to landing your dream job as

opposed to reminding someone to take out the garbage.

I once observed someone giving a really solid presentation, until he began speaking about his subject being involved in scandals and sex tapes. He presented it in a flat way, unfortunately. He said the words "scandals and sex tapes" in the same way that you would say a word like "door knob." He was trying to make a point, but his voice had no impact. What a miss!

Also, don't make the mistake of simply raising your volume. If all you do is raise your volume, now you're still being monotone, only louder. You've probably made it worse and more painful for the audience.

If you're not a loud talker, it doesn't necessarily mean you are monotone, so for those of you who speak more softly, your style may be perfectly fine, as is. I've witnessed many presentations where people have a naturally softer voice, but they still deliver a great presentation. The highs and lows in their pitch still exist.

EXAGGERATION

It's perfectly acceptable to dramatize your speech in parts that call for it. Just don't go overboard. Sometimes folks go in the other direction and end up too emotive. It comes across as disingenuous and as if you're overcompensating.

Allow me to indulge for a moment and qualify what I mean by excessive exaggeration. There used to be a perfectly fine word that unfortunately no longer seems to exist – "amazing." The word was useful and had purpose. Some things in life were amazing. Overcoming adversity, climbing Mount Everest, winning the little league championship when no one thought your kid's team ever had a chance, etc.

But the true meaning of that word disappeared, and now *everything* these days is A-MAAAZING! Getting a sandwich from the corner deli is apparently A-MAAAZING! See my point?

Please do yourself, me, and the entire world a favor and stop abusing that word. Pretty please? If everything is so A-MAAAZING, from you being proud that your dog had a healthy bowel movement to going to the Home Depot to buy a gallon of insecticide on a mundane Saturday morning, then what the hell is the purpose of the word?

DON'T SPEAK, SING

This is a little wonky, but maybe not. I think there is a lot of truth in it. I've always felt that some of my best presentations were when I was actually singing, well, sort of. I still practice this to continuously improve but when I do it, my audience seems to take a subtle notice to it.

I don't actually mean singing (I'm sure I'd be an awful singer if I ever tried). I mean speaking in a rhythm, almost as though it were a song. When your words flow from one to the next and it all sounds good, you sound good. Once again, the words become secondary.

George Carlin had a special ability to weave words and sing, instead of speaking, during many parts of his stand-up routines. Big Carlin fans like myself have noticed this.

I don't mean rhyming. I mean rhythm. These are two different things.

Take the lyrics of any great song and, assuming you're not a professional singer, sing them. Has anyone ever told you "don't quit your day job?" You may have butchered the song, right? The words out of your mouth are the same as the artist who has sold millions of copies and has fame and fortune. So what's the problem? The problem is that you don't know how to make those words sound good. You can, however, make the words in your presentation sound good.

Have you ever done karaoke? It can be a lot of fun. Some of us can't karaoke sing our favorite songs even when we know all the lyrics, and some of us are pretty good at karaoke because we know how to follow those bouncing balls that jump on top of each word. So learn how to make it sound pleasing.

That's what I mean by singing instead of speaking. You may have heard from time-to-time that some particular person "likes to hear themselves talk." It's almost always meant in the pejorative. Maybe in some ways that's not such a bad thing.

ENUNCIATION

About 15 years ago, I read a book on linguistics and found the information on enunciation both interesting and useful. Enunciation is the ability to articulate words in the best possible way. Don't confuse this with pronunciation. Pronunciation has to do with saying a word "correctly," according to the laws of English grammar as well as common use, etc. Enunciation means how the words SOUND coming out of your mouth.

YOUR "INTERVIEW VOICE"

I'm sure you've heard about your "interview voice," right? You know when you're getting on a scheduled call for a job interview and you answer the phone?

Your "hello" is *much* different than your "hello" after picking up the phone when your friend calls, right? When it's a job interview, you are so pleasant, dynamic, upbeat, positive, and all that good stuff. But it's the same exact word so what's going on?

That's enunciation!

UPSPEAK

It was suggested by an early reviewer that I add a few thoughts on upspeak (or uptalk). I briefly hesitated since I have no unique viewpoints on the issue, but nonetheless, it is worth mentioning briefly. One thing I will say is that I don't think this is solely attributable to young women, as many people claim. I see men do this too, and quite often, in New York City. But it might be fair to say that this is attributable to younger generations and millennials, in particular.

As you may know, upspeak is generally defined as completing your sentence as though it were a question. The idea stems from an unnatural need to make your sentiments seem positive (at all times) when it's completely unnecessary to do so.

It's about rising your intonation at the end of your sentence when it completely doesn't call for it. While some people may think this is normal (since we are conditioned that way, sadly), a lot of people will notice this and see it for what it is – a negative.

The trouble is that upspeak seems to have this need for approval or validation. And a lack of confidence. This can truly be a negative, since it seems as though you're putting something on the receiver when there is nothing additional to throw out there.

I had a really great time at the beach **this weekend(???)** So are you telling me that you had a really great time at the beach this weekend or are you not sure and want **ME** to add something to **YOUR** story to validate it?

There are plenty of good videos on upspeak on YouTube. Check them out!

CHAPTER EIGHT | STORYTELLING, AUTHENTICITY, AND BEING CONVERSATIONAL

While the bulk of this guide should help you navigate the ins and outs, I thought it was proper to talk a little bit about the guts of your presentation.

Although there's been so much written over the years, storytelling is still underrated, and I want to briefly share some of my own thoughts on this. I've touched upon some of these elements in various sections, but let's specifically talk a little about the value of storytelling in your presentations – no matter what type of presentation you make.

At the heart of storytelling is the idea that you're there for your audience and are taking them on a journey. In some way, you have the ability to alter your audience's psychological state.

This journey that I'm referring to can relate to any type of presentation, not just sales presentations, for instance.

All audiences have emotional needs and current emotional states. If you want to succeed, you need to understand both of these. The best way to understand this, I believe, ties back to authenticity and the heart of your message.

Another thing about storytelling is the necessity to "give away" more and more of your presentation as you go on and, consequently, more and more of yourself. When I'm in teaching mode, I do this all of the time. Granted, some people in the room understand it better than others, but it's your responsibility as the presenter to offer part of yourself but also transfer ownership of your story to them.

Not trying to get all metaphorical here, but a master chef can create the greatest dishes in the world, discuss them and show them to you. But, you won't feel as though you're part of the experience until the chef gives you a taste.

I do sincerely feel that the only way to truly have your audience embrace your words is to "give them" your words.

Remember, you don't always need to have people agree with a presentation you've made. If you can, great. But rather, ask yourself, "did they understand and absorb it"? Back to the chef analogy: you may not even have liked the dish, but the chef gave you a bite. You experienced it.

LANGUAGE

Authenticity in storytelling also depends on language you use. Use conversational language whenever you can. For example, instead of saying something like:

One must consider the ramifications of...

Try something like:

This is important because...

This is a better way of not only being more "real" but also less distant.

I'd also recommend, as appropriate, not to use "$50 words" when a "$5 word" will do just fine. I'm sure you've heard this before, but it's true. I'm not suggesting lowering the caliber of your vocabulary. In other words, don't use a steak knife to cut butter.

Why use "nefarious" if "evil" will do just fine? Why say "ascertain" if "figure out" works just as effectively? Actually, "evil," depending on your topic, may be a more descriptive word and better convey your meaning, anyway.

I hate to do this, but I'm going to reference politicians one more time. In general, voters resonate more with candidates who use "plain English." Use fancy words when it's called for. In most cases though, don't overdo it.

BE HERE NOW

To be here now means to be in the moment, which will also add to your authenticity. Give the impression that you're one of the audience, aware not only of yourself but also them.

Improv has some relevance here. You want to be able to respond rather than react. Reacting takes a lot more thought than responding does. I'm not telling you to not think before you speak, but responding is more natural, authentic, and sincere.

This is a valuable tool not only when managing questions, which we'll address in a separate section, but also as you're presenting the guts, or "meat", of your presentation.

When you think about storytelling, think about a time you read a bedtime story to a small child. You were most likely acting out the characters in the story, right? If you had to play several characters at once, you may have even done slightly different voices, change your pitch, etc. Storytelling is a dialogue, not a monologue.

When presenting, do the same thing. If you're talking about something that happened to you and a colleague or friend, play each character, so to speak. "Pretend talk" to that colleague or friend as you present, not to the audience. And vice-versa. It takes practice, but you'll see a creative side to you that you didn't even know existed.

I know I earlier discussed the power of a smile, so I don't want to come across hypocritical. Yes, there's power in a smile, but if you're embracing the storytelling technique, smile as the story calls for it; if you're discussing something perplexing, daunting, scary, sad, etc., try your best to adjust your facial expressions and body language to reflect that.

If you're just smiling the entire time, then you're defeating the purpose and can come across as inauthentic. If you're describing yourself shoveling snow, mimic the art of shoveling for your audience. If it was hard to shovel, pretend that you're strained and labored.

CHAPTER NINE | AGENDAS AND TRANSITIONS

I'd like to talk about agendas and transitions together because I think they're closely connected. I'll explain in further detail below, but it's first helpful to keep in mind that your overall presentation is made up of several chapters that create a story, like a book, or an overall message that consists of parts.

AGENDAS

It's important to provide an agenda of your presentation, and you generally have a lot of latitude in how you do it. It can be either explicit or implied, meaning it can be written (on a slide) or just spoken. I've never walked into a meeting room in my corporate life, or into a classroom in my teaching life, without providing an agenda. It's important to make sure you tell your audience why they are there and what you'll be talking about. Don't assume they already know. Sure, they may have a general idea, but be specific – it can only help. An agenda will not only reinforce or clarify the "what" – but it will also provide the "why." In other words, be concerned with what they'll get out of it.

Don't confuse this with a "presentation agenda" that literally lists out the specific topics in a timetable format, with hours, break times, lunch, etc. Those are perfectly fine, but they work better for an entire day of presentations. That's more of an itinerary.

An agenda should be clear. The "chapters" of your presentation should be listed in the simplest terms possible. If you decide to make an agenda slide and your topic is, for example, on the benefits of dual sourcing, you're probably trying to convince your company to move forward with a plan, and your agenda may look something like this:

Agenda

- State of the Category
- Current Challenges
- Alternatives and Options
- Overcoming Major Concerns
- Benefits
- Take-Aways/Next Steps

I would recommend always providing take-aways/next steps for business agendas. This is a better way of doing a conclusion since you're providing key action points by way of a summary. If you're presenting on something you've already placed into action and it's been successful, then you may want to conclude with calling it "Wins."

TRANSITIONS

Transitions can be tricky for both practitioners and students. In all fairness, books often explain transitions in ways that don't always make much sense. I like to think of transitions as linkages, connectors, or bridges. In short, they are the "set ups." I'll explain.

Transitions link one thought with the next. It's often been said (and perhaps proven, psychologically) that audiences remember the beginnings and endings of a presentation. Also, psychologists generally believe we have an attention span of approximately 17 minutes for any given topic. So, transitions help open and close each topic you're presenting, and they give meaning to what you have just said and are about to say.

Think of your overall presentation as a book. Books have chapters, and transitions are needed to connect each chapter. Or, think of a movie. A movie is made up of scenes. The transitions between scenes can be overt or nuanced, but all good, professionally-made movies have transitions that connect one scene to the next. You can also think of the parts/topics of your presentation as puzzle pieces. Think of when you did puzzles as a kid; you needed the puzzle pieces to fit together to recreate the image shown on the cover of box. You couldn't just force them into place.

There are many ways to do transitions. Some can be matter-of-fact, and some can be more nuanced. Here's an example of a very basic, matter-of-fact style:

Now that we've provided an overview of the 4Ps of marketing, let's discuss the importance of each of them.

Granted, this is very simple, but technically this is an acceptable transition. Why? You are telling your audience what you're concluding and what you'll be doing next. Again, you're connecting the pieces to create an overall story. You wouldn't want to give an overview of the 4Ps and then immediately get into detail of the first P (which is often Product). You never "set it up" for your audience. You owe it to them to do so.

Now, let's get a bit more complex. Here's an example of a more nuanced transition:

The "Historic-Future" or "Backwards-Forwards" Style:

The growth of the consumer internet in the 1990s was revolutionary. It created not only so much innovation but also new business platforms. But it's important to remember that while the internet was very exciting and created new value, in some cases it didn't. Technology just for the sake of technology isn't a guaranteed recipe for success. That will keep us grounded when we look at how to best manage opportunities with virtual reality (VR) and augmented reality (AR).

Here, I'm offering a bit of historical perspective to place these new opportunities into the appropriate context. I'm also "setting things up" for my audience.

The Rhetorical Question Style:

Let's say as a sales director you've given your sales team some information/facts on a new product. After you've given the information, you may ask something like:

Now how are we going to get our customers to see the brilliance of this new product?

Then you go into your suggestions for doing so.

While there are many transition styles you can use, make sure that you're "setting things up" as necessary. Also, remember that transitions are not optional. They are necessary. Again, you can think of them in different ways but remember that ultimately, they are the "connectors" in your overall story. They are smooth runway that allow you to move from one thought to the next. Without them, you'll be riddled with potholes, speed bumps, and detours.

TRANSITIONS WITH GROUP PRESENTATIONS

Group presentations are common in both industry and academic settings, and they also need transitions. Those transitions are easy to identify since typically each individual is given a sub-topic to present.

Most of the time, people in group presentations will make a basic transition and say something like this:

I'm now going to hand it off to Melissa.

There's nothing *wrong* with this, although I will admit it's pretty basic and not very impactful. There are more sophisticated transitions. I'll share a few examples that are not only more sophisticated and impactful but are dual purpose; you get two for the price of one. In other words, these examples also provide a nice summary/reinforcement/conclusion of what the previous speaker just presented.

Instead of simply providing the name of the next presenter, you can be impactful by doing something like this:

Now that we've shared why embracing social media like Instagram can really help improve your business, Melissa will walk you through how to execute some really exciting Instagram campaigns.

This is much more impactful, in my opinion. Also, this statement is versatile. In other words, it can be used by the outgoing presenter or the incoming presenter, which of course in that case, you replace "Melissa" with "I" or "We."

You can also try something like this, which in this case would be mentioned by the incoming presenter:

Wow! Mike just gave us three really compelling reasons why we need to increase security on our corporate IT platforms. Now I'll walk you through which one makes the most sense for you.

The incoming presenter provided a summary of what Mike just did –the three compelling reasons—and then segues into her section.

CHAPTER TEN | PRESENTATION INTRODUCTIONS

The most important thing to remember about introductions is your intended purpose. This can sometimes be independent of the overall objective of the presentation but be sure that your opening is not arbitrary.

Before we discuss some of the different techniques (the "what"), you'll need to understand your reason (the "why") for using them – the strategic part. No one really tells you these aspects, so I hope to give you a better understanding.

If you're going to start your presentation by asking a question, don't do it for trivial reasons. Even if you correctly execute the technique, it may not be effective. So, think about why you are asking the question and what you are looking to accomplish. Ask a question because you want the audience's buy-in and because you think this is the most efficient way to engage them.

On another strategic note, make sure that no matter which introduction technique you use, **it captures the overall tone of your presentation.** This is a bit nuanced and may take practice. Think of the opening credits of a movie or TV show. Generally, the opening credits will reflect the flavor of what's to come.

Ever watch Larry David's show *Curb Your Enthusiasm*? His opening is very short, but the light-hearted theme song sets the mood of the show. This is the same for Alfred Hitchcock movies, etc. You get the point.

Another thing I'll quickly share – and granted, this is probably reflective of my style – is that I'm not a big fan of shocking the audience. Some people will tell you that's a legitimate opening technique, and maybe so, but I don't see why you would ever need to shock your audience for attention. Shocking the audience, to me, seems as though you're trying to get attention for the sake of attention. You'll get attention by delivering something good.

I prefer openings that **captivate** my audience. They're more **sophisticated**, for the most part. Also, it can earn you the reputation of being a **thoughtful** presenter, regardless of the subject matter.

PRESENTATION OPENERS

Here are some techniques for openings that are useful and handy. I can't take credit for most of these, but I'll put my own spin on them for you.

The most common first:

1. Ask a Question

There are several ways do this effectively.

While this is probably the most common way to start a presentation, you should *truly understand* the purpose of this technique. Seriously. It's not as obvious as it seems. I've seen so many people use this technique and, either it wasn't clear why they used it, or they only used "half" of it. In other words, they ask a question but don't do anything with it.

You should anticipate how your audience will respond. If you ask a question, do "something" with it. For example, if you ask:

How many people here know about all of the atrocities happening to children in country X?

By asking this question you probably assume that the majority of the audience doesn't know the answer. If this is the case, you can then "finish" by transitioning into your overall theme. This is the proper execution.

Whether you are asking a question because you genuinely want feedback, or it's meant to be rhetorical, make it clear. It's fine if you want to make it rhetorical but make that clear in your tone and inflection. Here's an example of a rhetorical question used to open:

How many of us are tired of paying so much for Wi-Fi?

This would work well, rhetorically, because you can be reasonably assured that most, if not all, of the audience agrees. In this case, you don't need any weigh-in.

If by asking a question your intention is to get a response, make sure that you get one. Surprisingly, many presenters who want a response may not get one, especially with an unfamiliar audience. In short, make it clear that you want a response through your tone and body language. Alternatively, an easier route is to simply say "by show of hands…" This works very well and leave no ambiguity.

Another nuance part of the ask-a-question approach is to make sure you have a Plan B in your pocket, just in case it doesn't work out. It shouldn't happen too often, but there may be instances where, either you didn't research your audience, or you did research them but didn't accurately assess them. In either of these cases you might not get the response you hoped for. This is where having a Plan B is crucial. For example, let's say I expected the majority of my audience to familiar with marketing, but it turns out to be the opposite; almost no one knows about marketing.

By show of hands, how many people here have a basic understanding of marketing principles?

You were anticipating many hands but got only a few. Your Plan B in your back pocket can go like this:

Even better! Because the information I'm going to share with you today is especially essential for non-

marketing people. The last thing I'd want is for you to get tricked by advertisers.

You just got yourself out of a jam and, if you pull it off smoothly, the audience will never know. Again, this shouldn't happen too often, but it can, and you'll need to do a little adjusting on-the-fly to keep moving forward.

Have a plan B in your back pocket. Don't get tripped up!

2. Be Bold

This can be done several ways, but whichever way you do it, don't be afraid to start off with a bold statement. Obviously, you need to back up whatever you're asserting as you go through the presentation, but this style can help you to exude confidence from the start. You may use this technique with something like this:

Today, I'm going to give you three reasons why Hamilton (the play) is worth the hype.

This is bold for two reasons. First, you're articulating that you have three reasons as opposed to just reasons, and this specificity exudes a level of confidence because it demonstrates that you've thought this out in advance. Second, using a strong term like "worth the hype" implies that you acknowledge that some people think the play is overrated. You're going to provide three reasons why it's worth all of the fuss.

3. Say Something Provocative

If you use this technique, don't confuse it with shocking your audience. That's a separate technique that I won't get into, but you're not trying to shock your audience here. You're trying to make them THINK. Making a statement that may make your audience members a little uncomfortable or get under their skin may be fine. But it is your responsibility to understand how fine the line is between your intended effect and offending your audience.

Remember, you're trying to provoke thought, *not* insult. You may want to "poke the bear" a little but know how much is too much. For example, if you're doing a presentation in front of a group of rich donors, don't make general statements that are insulting to wealthy people.

4. Be Sincere

In 2014, when Ziauddin Yousafzai, the father of Malala Yousafzai, the youngest Nobel laureate winner, did a TED Talk on his daughter, he started his presentation with:

"In many patriarchal societies and tribal societies, fathers are usually known by their sons…but I'm one

of the few fathers who is known by his daughter, and I'm proud of it."

That's a pretty powerful statement. Plus, it gives you a strong glimpse of what he'll be talking about.

5. The "Stereotype" Approach

Another clever introduction technique is what I call the stereotype approach. With this technique, you're feeding the audience the typical stereotypes that you can reasonably assume they already associate with the topic. For example:

When you think of millennials, you probably think of them as:

- *Lazy*
- *Spoiled*
- *Entitled*
- *Selfish*
- *Always on their phones*

And that's probably just getting warmed up, right?

Then you can begin your presentation by trying to dispel the stereotypes. This works well in some cases since you are really providing your audience with instant credibility.

6. Instill Curiosity

This can be a clever intro technique if used in a situation that really calls for it. Don't confuse this with the ask-a-question technique. Here, you are probably asking a question, but you'll want to provide either portions of facts or figures, or perhaps purposely leave out some information for the time being. The idea here is to get the audience thinking about your question/statement on a deeper level. It doesn't have to be a deep topic, but you want to get them thinking. For example, let's say you started a presentation with:

What if, exactly one day before you were born, you can select some of your own attributes? Your race, gender, nationality. Remember, you're not born yet, so you have no preconceived notions. You're just selecting off of a menu. Would you do it?

OR

If you were able to meet any three people in the world, living or dead, who would they be, and why?

This technique can really evoke thought and curiosity, even if they haven't had enough time to think of all three names.

7. Share a Story

If you want to use this technique, make the story personal. It doesn't have to be about something tragic or sad. It can be though, if your topic/presentation calls for it. But there are many story types –inspirational, humorous, etc. Just keep in mind it shouldn't be too long. As we've discussed in a previous chapter, the wonderful details may matter to you, but not to everyone else. Again, make it personal, but relevant. Also, do your best to make sure the audience wants to hear it.

8. Quote Someone Famous

I'd be careful with this one. Yes, CAREFUL! You don't want to come across clichéd by using an over-used quote. This is just a suggestion, but I'd probably stay away from quotes and references such as:

Albert Einstein defined insanity "by doing the same thing over and over again and expecting a different result."

Don't get me wrong; it's a fine quote. But since so many people are already familiar with it, it's not all that impactful, in my opinion. Thousands of people around the world probably say that every day, so that's why I think it's not impactful or interesting.

9. "Process of Elimination"

I once saw a presenter start his intro with four photos of people and asked the audience to pick out the CEO of company X. While I don't remember the whole speech, I remember that this actually worked very well. It had purpose, wasn't too obvious, and wasn't elementary. This method has an interactive element that engages the audience from the start, without them having to work too hard.

10. Humor: Tell a Joke or Use Sarcasm

This is pretty self-explanatory, so you don't need me to offer an example. Just make sure that you're funny, as mentioned in chapter 7, and that it's appropriate for your particular audience. Sometimes sarcasm can be just as effective as telling a good joke. But if you're going to use sarcasm, I recommend that it be used appropriately; you should have proper inflection, tone, and body language. Facial expressions are also particularly important here. In other words, make sure you exaggerate, otherwise your audience might take you seriously, and your entire intro is ruined. I once had a graduate student use sarcasm at my expense to start her presentation:

FINALLY, *Al allowed us to pick our **OWN** topic for the last presentation of the semester! I'm so happy and felt like I was waiting **FOREVER**!*

It was funny! I have to admit I laughed a lot, too.

11. "Imagine"

This is a very interesting technique. I used it once and it really worked well. This technique requires the right inflection though, so when you start off a presentation with the word "Imagine" you'll need to do it in a sincere way. It will help to say it a bit slowly, giving great eye contact, and then pausing for a moment before you continue. For example:

Imagine (PAUSE)...imagine living on a deserted island, all by yourself, and cut off from the rest of the world...

If you see your audience's eyes light up, then you did it correctly.

CHAPTER ELEVEN | SLIDES

Let me start by saying that PowerPoints are NOT presentations. YOU are the presenter. A PowerPoint, no matter what kind of presentation it is, is designed to simply be your aid.

Two critical issues to share:

1. The Litmus Test

Most presentations today are done using PowerPoint or Keynote. I have what I think is a good litmus test for once you've completed your PowerPoint. Ask yourself this very honest question:

If I emailed someone this presentation, does the information I have here convey everything I need to share without needing to present it?

If the answer is yes, then you did *not* create a PowerPoint *presentation*. You've created a deck! If you're not familiar with the term, it's often used in corporate settings and is designed to be similar to reports that people read but in a "lighter," more concise and digestible way. In other words, if you answered yes, you've provided far too much detail and have "written" yourself out of a speaking role.

Why does the audience need you to present anything when you've already provided everything in deck? Not enough people ask themselves that question. So, if you're planning to present and you've created a deck, you'll need to go back and re-work your PowerPoint to make it a presentation.

2. Slides are for Your Audience, *Not* You

Too many presenters forget the true purpose of slides; they are for your audience. Also, remember that you don't really want your audience to read much of anything. *You want them to look.*

Additionally, you'll notice some presenters look at their slides far too much, or worse, they read word-for-word from the slide. Literally! This is likely an indication that they don't OWN their content.

Many books discuss how to prepare slides, and I generally agree with the advice. Things such as keeping slides clean and simple, not putting too much information, limiting the amount of text, using illustrations, tables/charts, etc. These are all good advice that I prescribe to.

MAKE NUMBERS MEANINGFUL

With regards to presenting numbers, I always stress that you should use analogies that your audience can relate to.

I'll take a page from one of my business heroes, Steve Jobs. Jobs always made numbers meaningful. Whether you're a finance person or not, don't be afraid to simplify numbers with analogies that make sense to a general audience.

I remember when MP3 players were gaining popularity in the late 90s. All the major players at the time, Sony, SanDisk, Creative Zen, etc., were marketing their devices with 256 mb, 512 mb, 1 gb, etc. of storage (yes, back in the late 90s that was a lot of storage!) But when *Jobs* unveiled the very first iPod in 2001, he simplified it by saying "1,000 songs in your pocket". It was simple. It was relatable.

Whether you're presenting to a technical audience that understands megabytes and gigabytes, simplifying it in a way that *everyone* can understand makes a lot of sense and can set you apart. Putting on my marketing hat for a moment, when the MP3 player was a new device, most people don't know what storage sizes meant. *Everyone* knows what 1,000 songs in your pocket means though, right? Your sweet little 95-year-old grandmother in 2001 would have known what 1,000 songs in her pocket meant.

A word to all of the finance folks reading this: making your numbers meaningful will not only make you a more dynamic presenter but can also set you apart from other finance professionals who just focus on the numbers. What good are the numbers if others can't understand and digest them.

PRESENTATIONS WITH NUMBERS

In addition to making numbers more effective from the standpoint of what was discussed above, it's also important to make your numbers visually impactful as well. While many of us (myself included) are trained to keep overall slide presentations to approx. 10 (exclusive of appendices), there are times where you can break the rules and the reward will be worth the risk.

For example, I've seen many presentations with basic financial numbers reported like this:

Revenue: $53B, Up 17% YOY

EPS: $2.34, Up +40% YOY

Operating Income: $11.5B, Up +33% YOY

While there's nothing inherently wrong with this, why not make 1 slide 3 slides and make it more impactful? Perhaps something like the following 3 slides?

$53B | +17%

Q317 $45B

Revenue

$2.34 | +40%

Q317 $1.67

EPS

$11.5B | +33%

Q317 $8.7B

Operating Income

Here, I think you'll agree; the numbers are large and impactful. And if you were thinking, why are the slide titles on the bottom as opposed to the top?

Well, my response is...who cares?! I think this looks fine and doesn't compete with the numbers. What will really happen if you put the slide title at the bottom, as long as it still makes sense and works? Is the TITLE POLICE going to come and arrest you?

IMAGERY — LOGOS, PHOTOS, ETC.

I also suggest using imagery when appropriate. You'll need to decide *when* it makes the most sense to use it. But images on a slide can often be more powerful than words on a slide, particularly when the images refer to something official. See Appendix A.

A PICTURE IS NOT ALWAYS WORTH A THOUSAND WORDS

I once saw a well-known businesswoman give a presentation on their life, a sort of mini biography, using PowerPoint, and included photos of herself. While imagery can be very powerful, showing a photo of yourself that arbitrarily coincides with a breakthrough moment in your career doesn't really add any value to the presentation. It's just a photo of you that happens to be from that time in your life. So what? It doesn't relate back to the point.

For example, if you finally saw career success come at age 50 and you show a picture of yourself blowing out candles on your 50th birthday cake, that's not very important. It's arbitrary. Your presentation is not about you turning 50. It's about you sharing that you achieved "real" success at 50. However, if you want to show a picture of yourself opening the door of the office you were finally able to rent, and you happen to be 50 in the photo, that can be effective. See the difference? I hope I'm not stating the obvious, but I thought it was worth mentioning since I know many people who can't make the distinction.

So, don't let it be arbitrary or come across as trivial. Make it meaningful and relevant.

SLIDE COUNT AND USING APPENDICES

I'd also suggest that you try to limit the presentation to 10 slides, if possible (excluding a cover slide). There are, however, some exceptions to this rule. But 10 slides are a good gauge. Create an appendix if you have additional information.

An appendix is great for two reasons. It shares additional detail with your audience if they ask for it afterwards, and it shows that you came well prepared. This can be particularly meaningful when the audience is comprised of your superiors.

A QUICK NOTE ON SLIDE ANIMATION

I'm a fan of slide animation but you should know how and when to utilize them. Be conservative and use them with purpose. In other words, don't have something flying across the screen just for the sake of it flying across the screen. You might find it fun, but your audience might find it distracting, trivial, or even juvenile.

Keep these guidelines in mind when animating your slides:

- Have separate bullet points and/or imagery appear one at a time when presenting ideas one at a time.
- Allow animation to mimic the ideas expressed on the screen. For example, if you are presenting either an outdated idea or something you don't

agree with in order to juxtapose it with something better, allow it to dissolve before introducing the better idea. That's where you can have "fun" with animation and it's completely appropriate.

- Both PowerPoint and Keynote allow you to set a time duration for animations. Make sure you test it out. Believe me. If you don't, your animation may look fine when you're creating it, but when you're presenting you'll end up wondering why it takes so long. If your bullet points are set to appear every second, drop it down to half a second.

- This might seem obvious, but make sure your animations are in the order you want them and that you didn't leave any "ghost" animations. If you animate bullet points on a slide but later revise the content, take out the animation for those "ghost" bullet points. If you don't, you'll get frustrated by clicking and having nothing happen. People will notice.

VIDEOS

Videos can either be great or lousy, so use them with purpose. There are many ways to utilize a video. Some presenters do it in the beginning, which is also one of the introduction techniques, some in the middle, and some at the end.

What you generally want to keep in mind is to limit the number of videos you use. Recognize when you're either playing too many videos or when your videos are too long. A few quick rules-of-thumb to help with this:

Use one video for every 10-15 minutes and do your best to keep each video under 90 seconds. Of course, there are exceptions, such instructional videos, etc. But for most presentations, you probably want to stick to this rule as your guide.

Unless you're using a video as part of your introduction, you'll need to provide some type of transitions to it. We spoke about transitions in an earlier chapter, so think about how to incorporate those principles. Before starting the video, tell your audience what they're about to watch. After, explain its relevance. That will go a long way in making your videos far more effective. If you're using a video as an introduction, then provide a combination of what/why after it ends.

A QUICK NOTE ON SOUND EFFECTS

If you're going to use sound effects, great. But if something that is particularly attributable to just one person on the planet, include a clip of the actual sound as opposed to trying to mimic it. I take nothing away from any talents you may have as an actor, singer, etc. I've had them all in my classes over the years, including a trained opera singer. But I am a fan of the "real McCoy," as they call it. For example, if you're giving a presentation on Donald Trump and you want to use his famous "You're

Fired" line, play a clip of him as opposed to mimicking it. As good of an actor you may be, the best person to play Donald Trump is Donald Trump.

With the ability to connect conference room audio to your personal devices, creating, uploading and playing different types of audio should be relatively easy.

A QUICK NOTE ON HANDOUTS TO YOUR AUDIENCE

Personally, I'm not a fan of handing out printed version of my presentation to the audience and, frankly, I never understood this. You're probably reading this and thinking, "it helps people follow along and take notes." I get that, but I'm still not a fan.

When you hand out a printed version, the audience spends too much time looking down, flipping pages or looking ahead rather than giving you the attention you deserve. If the audience wants to take notes, they can do so on their own without a copy of your slides. As mentioned earlier, if you are going to provide a hardcopy of the slides, do it at after. Alternatively, you can tell the audience that the slides will be available later on via email or saved on a shared drive, etc. My guess is this will alleviate some anxiety for those who tend to take lots of notes.

For those of you concerned about the environment, not printing your slides for handouts saves trees and probably saves an assistant from doing work that s/he doesn't really need to do. Most people throw out the handouts anyway.

A QUICK NOTE ON USING COLORS

While some of you may like to get creative with their slides, try not to go too far with choosing colors that aren't appealing to most people. Remember, slides are not for you; they are for your audience. So, slides with colors that are too rich or distracting can be unappealing. Aesthetic matters to your audience.

I'd also suggest that you keep colors to a minimum. Have some fun but keep them conservative.

A QUICK NOTE ON SAMPLES/VISUAL AIDS

Samples and other types of visual aids to hand out to the audience to touch and feel are great, but execution is important.

If, for example, you have to give a presentation on new fabrics and you have samples, this is opportunity to pass out swatches, but be sure to do it as the presentation is happening. If you have a somewhat large audience to have multiple swatches and ask someone to help you pass them out to rows, etc. This is for obvious reasons. You wouldn't want to move on to the next fabric while the previous swatch is still being passed around because the audience won't really be paying attention. Having someone else provide multiple swatches of each fabric *as you are presenting* will be more time efficient. Also, the audience will have seen and felt swatch 1 by the time you are finished speaking about it, and you will both be ready to move on to the next.

For other types of presentation where samples are helpful, it may be better to hold off until the end. Just be sure that during the presentation you tell the audience that you will be sharing samples at the end. This will hopefully alleviate the logistical nightmares that could result. I've seen in many corporate presentations where either no one was paying attention or people are busy trying to pass along a sample to the next person. This can be quite distracting and frustrating.

One last thing about preparing your slides. Again, forgive me for bringing up a basic issue, but make sure that you're using a large enough type font. Your type font may look large enough on your computer, but most of the time it isn't. So, in addition to keeping information on slides to a minimum, make sure to use a type font that uses enough space on the screen. Somewhere between 35 to 45-point is a general guideline.

CHAPTER TWELVE | DECIDING WHEN TO DO A PRESENTATION WITHOUT SLIDES

It's been said that Amazon CEO, Jeff Bezos, doesn't use slides. This is pretty common, so I think there's some value in discussing this.

Before we go any further, I'd like to unapologetically state that I don't at all subscribe to the belief that one's decision to give an entire presentation without visuals depends on the size of the audience. I don't believe this is a valid consideration. That's the type of guidance you find on the internet and is mainly technical in nature. Remember, this guidebook is about strategy, and the important nuances of presenting that I believe aren't given enough attention.

Think of the days before PowerPoint and Keynote. They weren't *that* long ago. There were great presentations, pre-software. You may call a presentation without slides a speech as opposed to a presentation, but that's fine.

One of the major benefits to not using slides is that your audience gives 100 percent of their attention to you. Some people may not like that. I get it. But, if you're confident and it makes sense, this might be a great opportunity for you.

Since we already established that slides are not for you, but instead for your audience, you should consider not using them when they won't actually benefit to your audience. Don't reduce this decision down to simple demographics. In other words, don't think that if you're presenting to an older audience you shouldn't use slides. Demographics should not factor into this decision.

Here are some situations that may make sense for presenting without a slide show:

- Your *authenticity* matters more than anything else.
- When your command of the subject matter is so deep that you can provide the information simple terms.
- When your storytelling skills are stronger than what any visual cues could offer.
- When audience interaction is key.
- When there are no actual numbers for the audience to digest or necessary images for the audience to see i.e. products, flow charts, etc.

Another way to look at this is: if you generally deliver strong presentations with slides but you begin to notice that your audience doesn't rely on them and instead focuses on you, this is a good indication that you don't need them.

This is a good opportunity to quickly revisit stand-up comedians. I don't think there is a single stand-up comedian that has ever used slides or visual aids consistently during their act. That would be silly, I know. But, if we look at this on a deeper level, the audience is there for the comedian's jokes – all delivered with use of his mind, body language, and the word out of his mouth. Stand-up is an area where there is nothing that the comedian could put on a slideshow that he can't show with his body language and facial expressions; there is nothing he would need to share with the audience that his couldn't voice.

So, the take-away here is this: First, be honest with yourself about your presentation skills. Second, if visual aids will not make you more effective in carrying out the objective of your presentation, then most likely you don't need a slide show.

Besides, think about all the good faith you'll receive from the audience. You'll begin to build a reputation for being a strong and *natural* speaker.

CHAPTER THIRTEEN | HANDLING QUESTIONS

Not all presentations allow for questions from the audience, but many do. Some people choose to take questions during the presentation, and some at the end of their presentation. I'll address this a bit later, but first allow me to provide some advice on how to handle them in general.

My best piece of advice is to anticipate what questions you'll be asked. This is not difficult for most topics if you own your topic and if you understand who your audience is. You may get thrown a curve ball now and then, but that's few and far between.

REPACKAGING QUESTIONS

Handling questions can be a bit complicated. There may be a time when the person asking a question doesn't necessarily know *how to ask* it. This is where you'll need to repackage.

Two main reasons for repackaging:

1. Making sure *you* understand the question.

Sometimes you may not be sure whether you understand the question. The questioner may be unable to completely articulate what he/she is thinking, or perhaps you simply don't understand the question being posed. Don't guess. It only takes a few seconds to re-ask the question. You can mention that you don't completely understand the question or say "let me make sure I understand your question" before re-asking. This is better than giving a response that hasn't answered the question; not only have you wasted time, but you answered something unnecessarily and revealed (somewhat) an inability to connect with the audience. Believe me when I tell you that others can tell. One thing to note: when you repackage a question, whether it's because of the asker's inarticulation or your own lack of comprehension, try not to sound patronizing.

2. The question being asked is one that you're confident *you* understand, but you're not sure the rest of the audience understands.

In this case, you want to simplify and repackage the question so that everyone else can also understand before you provide an answer. There may be people in the audience who either had the same question (but it wasn't clear from the way it was asked) or were confused by the question and were glad you clarified it. By repackaging, you ensure that everyone understands the question and the response.

ZOOM IN, ZOOM OUT

One important lesson I've learned is to address the questioner clearly and pointedly initially (since it's their question) before including to the entire audience.

Granted, this can be a bit tricky. Assuming most of you have a smart phone, think of this as zooming in and out of your phone by pinching the screen.

When someone asks a question, provide them razor-focused attention (zoom in) with your body language and listening skills. If the answer is a bit lengthy, or there is a counter- or follow-up question, you'll need to zoom out and address the rest of the audience at some point. You don't want to play "ping-pong" with one person and alienate the rest of the audience. Make sure that at some point your body language and eye contact are as such (looking around and moving back or slightly away) that you address everyone. This takes a little practice but can be done.

BE A LEADER

This is probably one of the few times I'd ever recommend that you to ignore your audience. If someone asks a question that others in the audience are annoyed by (they scoff at, roll their eyes, laugh or use body language that makes the questioner uncomfortable), my suggestion is to address the question by giving the asker your full attention. This means you face and speak directly to him/her. I've experienced this with students in my class several times and I've always felt bad. Again, ignore the audience by providing the questioner razor-focused attention through your eye contact and body language.

Give that person the attention that they deserve. Show that you care, even if you don't. Remember, perception is key. Also, try not come across as patronizing or condescending. If people scoff or rolls their eyes when a question is asked, it's your responsibility to be a leader and handle the situation respectfully.

WHEN TO TAKE QUESTIONS

You can take questions at the end or during the presentation. There are pros and cons to both and I'll address them concurrently.

The advantage of waiting until the end is that you don't lose any control or direction during the presentation. This approach may suit presenters who are a bit more linear and feel as though they will lose momentum if interrupted. Sometimes, depending on how your presentation is organized, it's *better* to wait i.e. if it's structured in a particular sequence that builds as you go. Don't get derailed by questions.

The main drawback to this, though, is if the audience needs clarification on a particular point. They may be unable to follow along if a certain piece is unclear. That would be a failure on your part.

Another drawback is that audience members may feel frustrated that they had to wait. Perhaps they won't ask a question they had earlier because they feel it's no longer "relevant" because the context has shifted.

A third concern with holding off until the end for questions is that you eliminate interaction with your audience. As a spatial presenter, I have always felt that allowing questions during a presentation enhances the overall quality of the presentation for two reasons.

First, it serves as a check point for you and your audience, particularly if you've just touched on a complicated point or concept. Simply asking, "does anyone have any questions so far?" can help you gauge if the audience is keeping up.

Additionally, you may be asked questions you hadn't previously thought about. Even if you're well prepared, you can't think of everything on your own. It's just not possible. Holding off until the end denies you the opportunity to enhance the overall dynamic of your presentation.

CHAPTER FOURTEEN | PRESENTATION CONCLUSIONS

Many of you aren't aware just how important conclusions are. As I said in an earlier chapter, we remember beginnings and endings, so conclusions should tie everything together and be impactful. Make it brief but make it meaningful.

About 15 years ago, I was given a piece of advice about conclusions that I'll never forget. Ironically, it's one of the most commonly used endings. *Never* end your presentation with "that's it." It's probably *the* worst ending of all time. Here's why: it's almost as if you are telling your audience that you don't care, and that you were too lazy to think of something better. It lacks substance. It lacks meaning. It's just all-around lousy.

As general rule of thumb, conclusions ought to be one of these:

- Memorable
- Personal
- Dramatic
- Emotional
- Funny

Of course, you should put your own twist on these, but here are some general guidelines:

- *The struggle continues, but with your support, it gets a little easier. Seriously consider contributing today.*
- *This university gave me so much when I was a student here X years ago. And now (PAUSE) it's my turn to give back.*
- *In the immortal words of Chuck D, "Don't Believe the Hype."*
- *Would you have ever thought that a homeless person at age 50 would have been able to turn his life around?*
- *So, remember, the only way to achieve equal rights for all is when women AND men strive towards equality TOGETHER.*

REFERENCING INSTEAD OF QUOTING

Some people like to quote someone famous in their conclusion. There's nothing wrong with this, but a reference to someone may work better than an actual quote. It provides the best of both worlds. It evokes the spirit of a famous/historical figure but remains authentically *yours*.

When I teach a large class (this generally works a bit better with larger classes), I give a small speech at the end of the last day. The speech is general, and I give it to both my undergrads and graduate students. I'm basically saying my "goodbye" and wishing them well for their future. I normally end with something inspirational from Gandhi, Freud, or someone else (pick someone that matters to you) and I choose two things attributable to that person and then top it off by saying:

And now… (PAUSE) I wish those two things for you… (PAUSE) thank you.

I reference a person without quoting them. I say "**I** wish those two things for you…" The ending is **mine**, not someone else's. See what I mean? It usually lands a heartfelt applause. It works well.

If you can't think of anything, or the nature of your presentation just doesn't call for any of the above – and I'm willing to concede that there may be a few presentations that simply don't – then at least give an enthusiastic "thank you!"

If you can't come up with anything clever and want to keep it simple and sincere, these are so much better than "that's it."

- *Thank you so much for your time.*
- *You've been a great audience, thanks again for having me.*
- *I can't tell you how much your time today means to me.*

I think you get the point.

The bottom line here is that you want your conclusion to correlate with your introduction, in some meaningful way. Even if you plan to have a

Q&A session immediately afterwards, I suggest to still have an actual conclusion.

RECAPS VS. CONCLUSIONS

When I offered a sample agenda in an earlier chapter, I suggested using "Takeaways/Action Points" in business meetings. I don't want to quibble over semantics, but I consider that a recap more than a conclusion.

Which one you use will depend on the nature of your presentation, and you'll have to use your best judgment. Be mindful of what your objectives are. Here, it may help to ask yourself some of the same questions you asked yourself earlier: "What am I trying to accomplish?" Or perhaps ask yourself some new questions: "Would reminding the audience of key points help to drive the point home?" "What impression would I like to leave the audience with?"

APPENDIX A | SLIDE EXAMPLES

The following are examples of how you can improve your overall presentation by enhancing the effectiveness of your slides. Many of you are probably much more creative than I am, so the following examples are just starting points to help illustrate the concepts I discussed. Of course, modify and add your own flair as needed.

1A. CHARTS INSTEAD OF BULLET POINTS

Let's start off with some basics. In general, sharing numbers works best in chart form as opposed to bullet points or lists. A chart can give not only give your numbers some "life," also provide a full view/understanding of what's happening *in context*. For example, instead of presenting information like this:

Q1 Sales

- Personal Care – 23%
- Home Fragrance – 15%
- Electronics – 18%
- Apparel – 35%
- Housewares – 9%

Try something more like this:

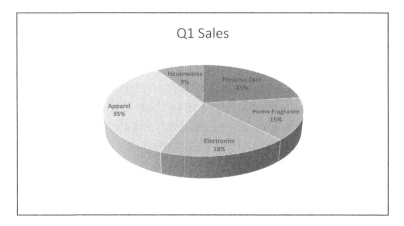

1B. IMAGERY INSTEAD OF BULLET POINTS

Sometimes, images can have much more impact than bullet points. Bullet points are not "wrong," but when the information relates back to something specific, a visual reference may work better. For example, if you're preparing a slide on someone who has won several awards, instead of doing this:

Awards Received

- Communicator of the year- PRWeek
- 100 most influential Hispanics
- Ranked 18th in 100 top CEOs worldwide

Try using the imagery and logos of the magazine, corporations, etc. (As of this early edition, I haven't yet received permission from the respective logo owners and therefore the slide example is omitted – but please remember, you can generally use logos without permission for non-commercial purposes, under fair use).

You don't want to overdo it and include arbitrary images, so use your best judgment.

1C. EXCERPTS FROM EXISTING TEXT

Sometimes it makes sense to quote, verbatim, either a statement or numbers, etc., straight from a press release. In cases like that, providing you don't need to show the rest of the press release, avoid simply highlighting the portions you want to stress because it's too hard to read. For example, instead of this:

You may want to instead try this:

In this case, you don't have any unnecessary text and you're focusing on only what is relevant. No need to highlight anything here, either. Don't worry, your audience, colleagues, etc., will believe the authenticity of the info and won't think that you've plagiarized info., "doctored" it, etc. I know I'm probably breaking so many grammar rules, but these excerpts don't have to grammatically perfect. Also, notice that in the slide header I added "From" to make it more consistent with excerpts instead of full text.

1D. TIMELINES IN VISUAL FORM

Timelines are a great way to express historically rich information in an aesthetic and linear way. You see this often in magazines and other publications. Be sure to make them simple and large enough to read. For example, instead of this:

Internet Firsts

1971 – the first email
1985 – the first domain
1991 – the first web page
1995 – the first Amazon order
2003 – the first Skype message
2004 – the first Facebook profile
2005 – the first YouTube video
2006 – the first Tweet
2010 – the first Instagram post

---

*You may want to try something like this:

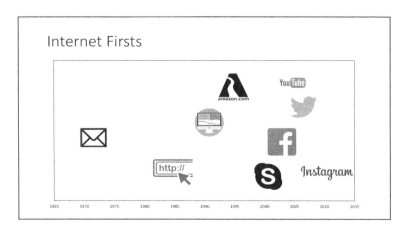

Internet Firsts

In the example here, notice that I created a timeline from 1965 to 2015 with increments of 5 years. This timeline is not precise, but it doesn't matter. Depending on the point you're making, it doesn't have to be.

Also, take note that I purposely set this up so that, visually, your audience can tell that nothing exciting really happened from the early 1970s to the mid-1980s. I'm making a subtle point by way of a visual. Also, notice that things began to really pick up in the early 2000s, hence why the graph looks pretty crowded post 2000.

*Amazon, Skype, Facebook, YouTube, Twitter, and Instagram are trademarks of their respective owners.

1E. USING UP SLIDES WITH ONLY "THANK YOU" OR "ANY QUESTIONS?"

I'm not trying to be a jerk but when you do a slide like this:

148

THANK YOU!

ANY QUESTIONS?

You're not adding much of anything. Sure, adding a slide at the end of your PowerPoint doesn't cost you anything (although it can if you print 50 copies of the presentation), but it just seems unnecessary. I think you can say "thank you" without the aid of a slide.

Instead, why not use imagery that aligns with your overall theme and supports your conclusion?

APPENDIX B | FAMOUS SPEECHES

I thought it might be helpful to share a list of famous speeches that may inspire you. These days, you can find almost anything on YouTube and the internet in general. Since links change over time, I'll just share the speech names and you can find them on your own. Most of these speeches are historical events and some are from famous movies. Inspiration can be drawn from either famous speeches or movies, so don't count out the movies.

Note, the list here is not exhaustive. There are so many more that deserve to be on this list, but I chose speeches that have at least an original audio component or video; reading a famous speech may not be as valuable as "witnessing" it either through audio or video.

Franklin D. Roosevelt's D-Day speech

Dr. Martin Luther King's "I Have a Dream" speech

Nelson Mandela speeches (various)

Winston Churchill's "Now We Are Masters of Our Fate" speech

Bill Clinton's 1992 Presidential victory speech

Ronald Reagan's speech when the Challenger space shuttle exploded in 1986

Ronald Reagan's "Remarks at the Brandenburg Gate"/"Tear Down This Wall"

John F. Kennedy's Inauguration speech

Malala Yousafzai's acceptance speech as the youngest Nobel Laureate

Lou Gehrig's "Goodbye" speech at Yankee Stadium, July 4, 1939

Al Pacino's "locker room" in *Any Given Sunday* and "courtroom" in *Scent of a Woman* speeches

Steve Jobs' 2005 Stanford University commencement address

Maya Angelou's 1992 Spelman College commencement speech

BIBLIOGRAPHY

This bibliography is by no means comprehensive. It's designed to be selective, and hopefully provide credit where its due. Much of this guide comes from my scratch notes and not formal research. Since the flavor of this guide has always been casual, the bibliography is also reflective of that.

Chibana, Nayomi. *12 Presentation Hooks Used by the Best TED Presenters*. Retrieved from http://blog.visme.co/how-to-start-a-presentation

Mercedes-Benz USA. (2018, July 3). *Mercedes-Benz USA reports June sales of 29,125 units* [Press Release]. Retrieved from https://www.media.mbusa.com/releases/mercedes-benz-usa-reports-june-sales-of-29125-units?firstResultIndex=0&sortOrder=PublishedDescending

Munter, Mary, and Lynn Hamilton. *Guide to Managerial Communication: Effective Business Writing and Speaking.* New Jersey: Pearson, 2013

Rose, Charlie. (2000). George Carlin Interview. Retrieved from https://www.youtube.com/watch?v=IJpyJeynU_E

TED. (2014, December 4). *Matt Abrahams: Think Fast, Talk Smart: Communication Techniques* [Video file]. Retrieved from

https://www.youtube.com/watch?v=HAnw168huqA
&t=11s

TED. (2013, June 25). *Patrick Munoz: What is Upspeak?* [Video file]. Retrieved from https://www.youtube.com/watch?v=2RjPOUZkLfU

Wikiquote contributors, "George Carlin," *Wikiquote,* https://en.wikiquote.org/w/index .php?title=George_Carlin&oldid=2465378 (accessed August 17, 2018).

Wikipedia contributors, "Injection molding," *Wikipedia, The Free Encyclopedia,* https://en.wikipedia.org/w/index.php? title=Injection_moulding&oldid=900147114 (accessed August 19, 2018).

Wikipedia contributors, "Internal combustion engine," *Wikipedia, The Free Encyclopedia,* https://en.wikipedia.org/w/index.php? title=Internal_combustion_engine&oldid=857304606 (accessed June 26, 2018).

Wilson, Karen; Korn, James H. (5 June 2007). "Attention During Lectures: Beyond Ten Minutes". *Teaching of Psychology*. 34 (2): 85–89.

Al Golzari is a senior-level consumer product professional with 15+ years' experience in product development, innovation, sourcing, and vendor management along with 10+ years of adjunct teaching experience at all levels, including executive MBA. He has worked at various companies including LBrands, Target, and Macy's, along with consulting work.

A native of northern New Jersey, he currently resides in New York City.

Made in the USA
Middletown, DE
27 June 2020